Globish

The World Over

全球语

沟通全世界

By Jean Paul Nerrière
and David Hon

让·保罗·内里埃

大卫·洪

著

A book written IN Globish

(Translation by Luo Xi)

一本用全球语写的书

罗　希

译

Globish The World Over

© 2009 Jean-Paul Nerrière and David Hon

(Translation by Luo Xi)

US Copyright Registry Case #1-206193066

ISBN: 978-0-9842732-8-7

全球语 沟通全世界

© 2009 Jean-Paul Nerrière, David Hon

罗 希

译

US Copyright Registry Case #1-206193066

ISBN: 978-0-9842732-8-7

International globish Institute

Table of Contents

目录

Foreword for the Chinese Translation

Globish The World Over is among the few books that go to the readership with side-by-side translation. It means that the original text and the Chinese translation can be read next to each other on every page. Thus this book fills a double function. On one hand reading only the right side, the Chinese translation, the book can give information, and perhaps amusement, to those who speak little or no English. They are interested in an amazing process that is happening in front of the eyes of people in this age: The world has found a common language. It will help all people to communicate with each other, and this language is being called *Globish*.

On the other hand, the side-by-side translation provides an opportunity to the learners of English -- or perhaps learners of Chinese -- to use

中文版前言

在《全球语：沟通全世界》这本书中，读者们会发现原文和译文并排显示。这意味着读者可以在每一页中同时阅读原文和汉语译文。因此，这本书就拥有两个功能：一方面，如果只阅读右边的汉语译文，那么这本书可以给那些会一点儿英语或不会英语的读者们提供知识，或作为一种消遣。令读者们感兴趣的是这个时代的人们正在见证的一个惊人的变化过程：全世界的人们发现了一门通用语言。这将有助于人与人之间的沟通，而这门语言就叫做*全球语*。

另一方面，英汉对照的格式使得英语学习者或汉语学习者可以将此书作为学习语言

this book as a kind of language coursebook. During the translation, we paid special attention to following the grammatical structure and the phrasing of the original text. It is portrayed accurately to the extent the different structure of the Chinese language allows us to do so. We hope this method will provide a real opportunity -- in a real language environment -- for the learners of English to follow and recognize elements of English they have learned in school.

的教材。在翻译的过程中，我们特别注意遵循原文的语法结构及措辞。由于汉语和英语的结构不同，我们在允许的范围之内对原文稍加修改。我们希望这样可以在真正的语言环境中为英语学习者提供一个良好的机会，使其能够领悟并意识到他们在学校所学的英语要素。

Beginning

What if 50% of the world badly needed a certain useful tool, but only 5% could have it?

Someone would find a way. For example, to solve the problem of talking, they gave us handsets for little money and charge us by the minute. But that only does part of it. What will we *say* to each other?

The English language seems to be the most important communication tool for the international world. But now it must be a kind of English which can be learned quickly and used very easily - not like Standard English. The people who know a little are already using what they know. It works for them - a little. But... they often have families and jobs. They

卷首语

如果世界上 50%的 人都急需一种有用 的工具，但是只有 5%的人能拥有它， 怎么办？

有些人找到了解决的办法。例如，为了让我们随时可以交谈，他们以很低的价钱将手机卖给我们并按分钟收费。但是这并没有从根本上解决问题，我们互相之间该*说些什么*呢？

英语似乎是目前国际上最重要的沟通工具。但是与标准英语不同，作为沟通工具的英语必须简单易用。那些掌握了少量英语的人们已经在竭尽所能的使用英语了。但是这对他们来说却收效甚微。因为这些人通常都有家庭有事业，所以他们没有足够的时间或金钱来学习

cannot spend enough time or enough money to learn all of English. And English speakers think these people will "never be good enough" in English. It is a problem. We think Globish is a solution.

Globish has a different name because it is a very different way to solve the problem of learning English. By the standards of the Council of Europe Framework of Reference for Languages (page 64):

> *(Globish speakers) will use an amount of English that makes understanding between non-native speakers and native speakers. They will produce clear, detailed writing on a wide range of subjects and explain their thoughts, giving good and bad elements of various ideas.*

This book is *about* Globish and to demonstrate its value, we'll write this book for you *in Globish*.

所有的英语。而以英语为母语的人又认为这些人的英语"永远都不够好",这就成了一个问题。而我们认为全球语可以解决这个问题。

全球语拥有一个不同的名字是因为它通过一个与众不同的途径来解决英语学习的问题。根据欧洲议会制定的欧洲共同语言参考标准（第64页）：

（全球语的使用者）能够让非英语母语人士及英语母语人士理解他们所说的英语。他们可以以书面形式就广泛的题材清楚的，详细的表达并解释自己的想法，可以分析各种不同观点的好坏之处。

这本书*讨论的*就是全球语，并且为了证明其价值，我们将用*全球语*来为您写这本书。

Part 1
The Problem
with Learning
English

第一部分
英语学习中的问
题

Chapter 1
Many, Many Languages

A hundred years ago, most human beings could speak two or more languages. At home they spoke a family language. It could be the language their parents spoke when they moved from another place. In many cases, it was a local variation of a language with different words and different pronunciations, what some people might call a dialect or patois. Most villages had such languages. People learned family languages, village languages and sometimes other languages without any problems.

A century ago, for most people the world was not very big, perhaps as big as their nation. They learned their national language and then could communicate with the rest of their world.

第一章
很多，很多种语言

100年前，大多数人都会说两种或多种语言。在家里的时候，他们说家族的语言。这有可能是他们的祖先在从另一个地方迁徙过来之前所说的语言。在许多情况下，这是一种由于地域差别而形成的，带有不同词语及不同发音的语言变体，也就是人们通常所说的方言或土话。大多数村镇都有这样的语言。那时的人们在学习家族语言，方言，以及其他语言的时候毫无困难。

一个世纪之前，对于大多数人来说世界并不是很大，或许对他们来说国家就是世界。他们学习了本国的语言就可以与世界上的其他人交流了。当时许

Many nations had at least one official national language. Many people in their villages also felt a need to speak the national language, and they would learn that national language in schools.

National languages made nation-wide communication possible. In some cases these started as one of the local dialects and were raised to the status of national languages. Or sometimes one "family" was more powerful, and required everyone to speak their way.

Today, the communication problem is the same. Just the scale is different. A century ago, their world was their country. Now their world is.... much more. Most people now speak a local language which is often their national language. Now they must communicate to the whole globe.

多国家至少都有一种官方语言。而村镇里的大多数人都觉得有必要说官方语言，而且他们也会在学校里学习官方语言。

一个国家的官方语言使得全国的人们可以互相交流。在某些情况下，一个地方的方言被提升至官方语言的地位。或者有时某个家族的势力更加强大，于是他们要求所有的人都说他们的语言。

现在，沟通的问题仍然存在，只不过范围不同罢了。一个世纪之前，人们的世界就是他们的国家。而现在他们的世界变得更加广阔了。目前大多数人只说一种语言，而且常常是他们国家的官方语言。但现在他们必须和全世界的人交流。

(From English Next)　(摘自 《英语走向何方》)

Non-English speaking to non-English speaking
74%

非英语母语人士之间的交流 74%

English to English 4%

英语母语人士之间的交流 4%

English to other countries 12%

英语母语人士与其他国家人士之间的交流 12%

Other countries to English 10%

其他国家人士与英语母语人士之间的交流 10%

So 96% of the international English communication takes place with at least one non-native speaker.

In this world, teachers say there are more than 6000 languages. In 45 countries, English is an official language. But not everyone speaks English, even where it is an official language.

Only 12% of the global world has English as a mother tongue. For 88% of us, it is not our first language, our mother tongue.

We know that only 4% of international communication is between native speakers from different English-speaking nations - like Americans and Australians.

所以在96%的使用英语的国际交流中，至少有一方是非英语母语人士。

老师们告诉我们世界上有超过6000种语言。而英语是45个国家的官方语言，但是即使是在这些国家里，也并不是每个人都会说英语。

世界上以英语为母语的人口只占世界总人口的 12%，而对于我们这样属于其余 88% 的人来说，英语既不是我们的第一语言，也不是我们的母语。

我们知道只有 4% 的国际交流是在不同英语国家人士之间进行的，例如美国人和澳大利亚人之间。

There is a story about a god and a Tower of Babel, where all men could speak to each other using just one language. In the story, he stopped the building of that special Tower.

He said (roughly):

"Look, they are one people, and they have all one language. This is only the beginning of what they will do. Nothing that they want to do will be impossible now. Come, let us go down and mix up their languages so they will not understand each other."

In the past, there have been many strong languages and attempts to create a common worldwide language. Some worked well, but some not all. The Greek language was used as the "lingua franca" in the days of the Romans. Non-Romans and others read the first Christian books in Greek. Modern Romans speak Italian, but until lately

圣经中有个关于上帝和巴别塔的故事，那时所有的人类都说同一种语言。故事中，上帝阻止了人类建造通往天堂的高塔。

耶和华说（生气的）：

看哪，他们成为一样的人民，都是一样的言语。如今既作起这事来。以后他们所要作的事，就没有不成就的了。我们下去，在那里变乱他们的口音，使他们的言语彼此不通。

——创世记 11:1-9（中文和合本）

过去有很多强势语言试图成为世界通用的语言。有些成功了，有些却没有。希腊语是罗马时期的通用语言。非罗马人和其他国家的人最初读到的基督教书籍都是用希腊语书写的。现代罗马人说意大利语，但直到最近天主教在宗教仪式

14

Catholics celebrated Christian ceremonies in Latin, the language of the ancient Romans.

French was the language of upper class Europeans for several hundred years. It was used for international government relations until 1918. Many thought it was clearly the best language for all international communication. Tsarina Catherine of Russia and Frederick the great of Prussia used to speak and write very good French, and made a point to use it with foreigners. A friendly competition took place at the king's court in France in 1853 to find the person who used the best French. The winner was not Emperor Napoleon the Third, or his wife Eugénie. Instead, it was the Austrian statesman Klemens Wenzel von Metternich.

About this time, in the Age of Reason, humans began to think they could do anything.

中仍然使用古罗马的拉丁语。

在过去的几百年中，法语曾是欧洲上流社会的语言。1918年之前法语一直是各国政府间交流所使用的语言。很多人都曾认为法语一定会成为国际间交流最好的语言。俄国女皇凯萨琳大帝（又称叶卡捷琳娜二世）与普鲁士国王腓特烈大帝的法语会话和书写能力都很强，并且坚持在与外国交流中使用法语。1853 年的一天，一场友谊竞赛在法国国王的庭院里展开，目的是为了决出谁的法语说得最好。最后胜出的人既不是皇帝拿破仑三世也不是他的皇后欧也妮，而是奥地利政治家克莱门斯·文策尔·冯·梅特涅。

大约从理性时代开始，人类认为他们无所不能。他们发现了

They discovered drugs that would cure diseases. They could grow food in all weather. Their new steam-ships could go anywhere without wind. So then some people thought: **How difficult could it be to create a new language, one that would be easy and useful for all people?**

可以治疗疾病的药物。他们可以在各种气候条件下种植粮食。他们发明的蒸汽船可以不依靠风力到达世界上的任何地方。因此，有些人寻思：**那么创造一门既简单而且所有人都可以使用的新的语言，又有什么难的呢？**

Technical Words

Chapter - people divide large books into smaller chapters

Dialect - a different way of speaking a mother tongue

Patois - a way of speaking in one region

Lingua franca - a Latin word for a global language

Pronunciation - the way we say sounds when we speak

International Words

Planet - a space globe that moves around the Sun

Chapter 2
Esperanto vs...the World?

Natural languages come from unwritten languages of long ago, in the Stone Age. They are easy to learn naturally but hard to learn as a student. That is why many people have tried to invent a simple language that is useful and simple to learn. Perhaps the most famous of these *invented* languages is "Esperanto." It was developed between 1880 and 1890 by Doctor Ludovic Lazarus Zamenhof. He was a Russian eye doctor in Poland. He said his goal was to create communication and culture-sharing among all the people of the world. He thought the result would be understanding by everyone. That would mean everyone would have sympathy with everyone else and this would avoid future wars.

第二章
世界语 VS 世界？

自然语言是由很久以前石器时代的没有文字的语言演变而成的。这些语言是很容易自然学会的，但是如果作为外语来学习的话会很困难。因此很多人尝试过发明一种简单实用易学的语言。或许在这些发明出来的语言中最著名的莫过于"世界语"了。它是在 1880 至 1890 年间由路德维克·拉扎鲁·柴门霍夫博士发明的。他是一位波兰籍俄国眼科医生。他说过他的目标是使得全世界人民互相交流与共享文化。他曾经认为结果会是每个人都达成谅解。也就是说世界上的所有人都会互相同情，而这将使未来

Here is a example of Esperanto:

En multaj lokoj de Ĉinio estis temploj de drako-reĝo. Dum trosekeco oni preĝis en la temploj, ke la drako-reĝo donu pluvon al la homa mondo.

Easy for you to say... perhaps. But there was one big problem with Esperanto. No one could speak it. Well, not really *no* one.

的世界避免战争。

以下是一篇世界语的例文：

En multaj lokoj de Ĉinio estis temploj de drako-reĝo. Dum trosekeco oni preĝis en la temploj, ke la drako-reĝo donu pluvon al la homa mondo.

或许看起来容易。但是世界语有个很大的问题：没有人会说。好吧，并不是一个都没有。

After more than a century, there are about 3 million people who can speak Esperanto. And that is in a world of nearly 7 *billion*

The 1st Esperanto book
第一本世界语书籍

people. Sadly, many wars later, we have to admit the *idea did not work as expected.*

For a while, Esperanto was an official project in the USSR, and in the People's Republic of China. It is long forgotten in those countries now. There are no Esperanto guides in the Moscow or

在世界语出现一个多世纪之后，大约有三百万人会说世界语。然而现在的世界人口已经接近七十亿了。令人遗憾的是，世界上仍然有战争，我们不得不承认这个想法*并不像当初期望的那样起作用。*

世界语在前苏联和中华人民共和国曾经是官方项目。而现在已经被遗忘很久。今天莫斯科和上海的火车站里再也没有世界语的标识引导乘客。我们现在只能想象如果当年前苏联选

Shanghai railway stations to help passengers find their trains. We can only wonder what the world would be like if the Soviets had chosen Globish instead…

There are still people who believe in Esperanto. They still have their "special" language. Sometimes Esperantists make news when they speak out against Globish -- using English, of course. Thus any major newspaper story about Globish and Esperanto clearly demonstrates that Esperanto is not working. And it helps show that Globish gives us an opportunity to have - finally - a real global communication tool.

择了全球语，那么今天的世界会是什么样子。

然而，仍然有人相信世界语。他们仍在使用他们的"特殊"语言。有时世界语的支持者们会制造新闻公开反对全球语——当然，他们使用的是英语。因此，所有主流报纸的报道都清楚地表明世界语已经被淘汰了。而且它还帮助我们认识到全球语最终有机会成为一个国际间交流的工具。

International Words
Million = 1,000,000
Billion = 1,000,000,000

Chapter 3
Thinking Globally

It would be difficult for all people in the world to have one official language. Who would say what that language must be? How would we decide? Who would "own" the language?

Most people today speak only their one national language. This is especially true with native English speakers. They observe that many people in other countries try to speak English. So they think they do not need to learn any other language. It appears to be a gift from their God that they were born ready for international communication. Perhaps, unlike others in the world, they do not have to walk half the distance to communicate with other cultures. Perhaps English IS the place everyone else must come to. Perhaps.... All

第三章
放眼全球

如果让全世界所有人都使用同一种官方语言的话，那将会很困难。谁能说一定是哪种语言？我们怎样决定呢？谁会"拥有"那种语言呢？

现在大多数人只会说一种本国语言。特别对于以母语为英语的人士来说，更是如此。他们注意到许多其他国家的人努力学说英语，因此他们认为自己不需要再学习其他语言了。这仿佛是上帝赐予他们的天赋，使他们自出生就具备了进行国际交流的条件。或许，与世界上的其他人不同，为了与其他文化进行交流，他们不需要付出努力。或许，每个人都确实需要学习英语。或许…其他所有人生来就不走运。但是*或许*事情并没那么简单…

others are unlucky by birth. But *perhaps* there is more to the story...

It does seem English has won the competition of global communication. Although it used to give people an edge in international business, one observer now states it this way:

> *"It has become a new baseline: without English you are not even in the race."*

So now the competition is over. No other language could be more successful now. Why is that?

The high situation of English is now recognized because communication is now global, and happens in one second.

There have been periods in history where one language seemed to have worldwide acceptance. But, in all these periods, the "world" covered by one of these languages was not the whole planet.

看起来英语赢得了国际交流语言的竞争。虽然过去使用英语的人在国际商务中占有优势，但是现在一个观察家这样说道：

"它已经成为一个新的基准，不会说英语的人甚至都没有成功的机会。"

所以现在竞争结束了。英语比其他任何语言都更为成功。这又是为什么？

英语的强势地位之所以为人们所认可是因为目前人们之间的沟通都是全球性，也是瞬时性的。

在历史上的不同时期，某种语言似乎得到了全世界的承认。但是，在所有这些历史时期中，这些语言所覆盖的"世界"并不是全球。

Chinese was not known to Greeks in the time of the Roman Empire. The hundreds of Australian languages were not known to Europeans when they settled there. Japanese people did not learn and speak French in the 18th century.

Then, much communication was a matter of time and distance. Now, for the first time, communication has no limits on our Earth. 200 years ago it took more than six months to get a message from Auckland, New Zealand, to London. In our global world, a message goes from Auckland to London in

罗马帝国时期的中国人并不知晓希腊语。当欧洲人移居澳大利亚时并不知道当地的上百种语言。18世纪时的日本人也没有学习说法语。

那时，大量的交流受到时间和空间的阻碍。而现在，世界上所有人之间的交流首次没有了限制。200年前，从新西兰的奥克兰捎个信到伦敦都需要超过半年的时间。在我们全球化的世界中，从奥克兰发送一条消息到伦敦只需要不到一秒钟。

less than a second.

As Marshall McLuhan said in his book *The Guttenberg Galaxy*, this world is now just the size of a village – a "global village." In a village, all people communicate in the language of the village. All nations now accept English as the communication for our global village.

正如马歇尔·麦克卢汉在他的《谷登堡星汉璀璨》一书中所说：现在的世界就犹如一个村庄——一个"地球村"。在一个村庄里，所有人都用村庄的语言进行交流。现在所有的国家都认可英语作为我们地球村的交流用语。

Some people dislike that fact a lot. They want to keep their language, and even to avoid English. And, there are people who do not care at all, and they do not see what is happening or what it means.

有些人很不喜欢接受这个事实。他们想要保留自己的语言，甚至要避免使用英语。而且还有人根本就不在乎，他们并不知道世界正在发生什么变化，也不知道这意味着什么。

Finally, there are people who accept it, and even benefit from it. Many Chinese, Spanish and German people realize their language is not global and so they are learning English. They speak about their wonderful culture in English but they also continue to speak their first language.

最终，人们接受了这一事实，甚至还从中受益。许多中国人，西班牙人，和德国人意识到他们的语言不是全球通用的，所以他们学习英语。他们用英语谈论自己灿烂辉煌的文化但同时他们仍然使用自己的第一语言。

We can be very confident this situation will not change.

我们可以坚信这种情况将不会

With all the people now learning English as a second language, and there will be no need to change. As in the past, people will speak more than one language as children.

Leading economic powers, such as China, Brazil, India, Russia, and Japan will have many people speaking English. No one is going to win markets now with military battles.

And no one will need to change languages, as used to happen. Now nations will try to win hearts and minds with their better, less expensive products. It is a new world now, and maybe a better one.

To communicate worldwide, these people will use varying qualities of English. But once they master "a reasonable amount" of English they will not want or need to require others to use their mother tongue. So English will certainly continue to be the most important international language. The economic

改变。既然现在所有的人都将英语作为第二语言来学习，那么也不需要再做改变。正如过去一样，人们从孩童时代开始就会说不止一种语言。

世界主要经济大国，如中国，巴西，印度，俄罗斯，和日本，将会有许多人说英语。现在没有人会通过发动军事战争来赢得市场。

而且人们也不需要像以前那样改变语言。现在所有的国家都试图用更好更便宜的产品来赢得人心。今天的世界已经不同了，或许它会变得更好。

在与全世界进行交流的时候，人们将会使用各式各样的英语。但是只要他们掌握了"合理数量"的英语，就会不希望也不需要其他人使用他们的母语。因此英语将仍然是最重要的国际语言。今后商界的精英们将能相当好的使用英语以至于不再需要其他辅助。每个人都

25

winners today or tomorrow will use their English well enough so that they don't need anything else. This "common ground" is what everybody will continue to agree on…

将会继续在这个"共同点"上达成一致……

Language Used In Business Communication
商务交流中使用的语言

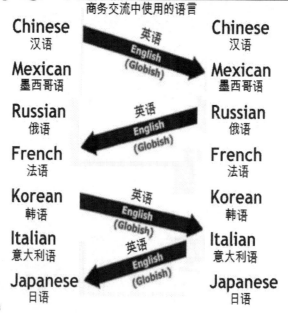

© David Hon 2008

Today, Mandarin Chinese is the language with the most speakers. After that is Hindi, and then Spanish. All three of them have more native speakers than English. But

尽管如此，还是会有很多人学习汉语或西班牙语或俄语。他们这样做是为了对其他文化增进了解。但是这对在全世界做生意不会有什么帮助。因为在

Hindi speakers talk to Chinese speakers in English and Spanish speakers communicate to Japanese speakers in English.

Everyone in this meeting will then agree to change back to English, because everyone there will have acceptable English.

世界任何一个地方的国际会议上，总有人不会说当地的语言。

到那时会议上的所有人都会同意换回英语，因为每个人都有一定的英语能力。

Still, many people will continue to learn Chinese or Spanish or Russian. They will do this to understand other cultures. But it will be of less help in doing worldwide business. In an international meeting anywhere, there will always be people who do not speak the local language.

They cannot use their own languages so they must use the most international language to do current business. That is why English is now locked into its important position the world over.

Sometimes we wonder if it is good that English won the language competition. We could argue that it is not the right language. It is far too difficult, with far too many words (615,000 words in the Oxford English Dictionary...and they add more each day.)

Too many irregular verbs. The grammar is too difficult. And most importantly, English does not have good

汉语是当今世界上使用人数最多的语言，其次是印地语，之后是西班牙语。所有这三种语言的使用者都比英语的使用者要多。但是印地语母语人士在与汉语母语人士交流时说的是英语，而西班牙语母语人士也是通过英语和日语母语人士交流的。

他们不能使用自己的语言，所以他们必须用最国际化的语言来做生意。这就是为什么英语会在世界范围内居于如此重要的地位。

有时我们怀疑英语赢得了竞争对我们来说是否是件好事。我们可以争论说英语并不是合适的语言，英语太难了，还有那么多的单词（牛津英语大词典收录了615,000个单词，而且每天都在增加。）

英语有太多的不规则动词，语法也很难。然而最重要的是，英语口语与书面语的联系没有

28

links between the written and the spoken language. Why do the letters "ough" have four different pronunciations ("cough, tough, though, through") Why is a different syllable stressed in photograph, photography and photographer? And why is there not a stress mark? Why doesn't "Infamous" sound like "famous?" or "wilderness" like "wild?" Why isn't "garbage" pronounced like "garage", or "heathen" like "heather"?

English was never expected to make sense to the ear. Pronunciation in English is a horrible experience when you have not been born into that culture. Yet it appears to sound natural to native English speakers.

Some languages, like Italian, German, and Japanese, can match written words to the way they are spoken. So it may appear unlucky for us that one of them did not win it all. Italian, for example, is a language where every letter,

规律可循。为什么"ough"这几个字母有四种发音？（"cough, tough, though, through"）为什么photograph与photography和photographer的重音不同？为什么单词没有重音符号？为什么"Infamous"和"famous"还有"wilderness"和"wild"听起来一点都不像？为什么"garbage"和"garage"还有"heathen"和"heather"读起来也不像？

英语一直以来都不是那么容易听懂的。如果你不是生下来就会说英语，那么学习英语的发音是非常痛苦的。然而这对于英语母语人士来说却很自然。

有些语言，如意大利语，德语，和日语的书写和读音是相匹配的。所以对我们来说这些语言没有赢得竞争可能是不幸的。例如，意大利语中的每个字母及每组字母的发音总是相同的。如果你手里有一份意大利

and every group of letters, is always *pronounced* the same way. When you are given an Italian document, you can *pronounce* it once you understand a limited number of fixed rules. In English you have to learn the *pronunciation* of every word.

Many English words are borrowed from other languages, and they sometimes keep their old pronunciation and sometimes not. English words cannot be written so the stressed syllables are shown. All non-native English speakers know that they may have to sleep without clothes if they try to buy "pajamas." Where is the mark to show what we stress in "pajamas?" So, the borrowed word "pajamas" would be better written as *pa-JA-mas*. In English you must learn exactly which syllable gets the stress, or *no one* understands you.

But Italian, German, or Japanese did not win the language competition.

语的文件，只要你掌握了数量有限的几个固定规则，那么你就可以*读出*这份文件。但如果是英语的话，你就必须学习每个单词的*发音*。

英语中的许多词语都是外来词，有的保留了原来的发音而有的却没有。英语词汇的书写方法并没有突出重音的位置。所有的非英语母语人士都知道如果他们想要去买"pajamas"的话，他们晚上可能就要光着身子睡觉了。那个显示"pajamas"重音的符号在哪里呢？那么如果将外来词"pajamas"写成pa-JA-mas就更好了。你在学习英语时必须清楚地知道哪个音节要重读，否则*没人*能够听懂你说的话。

但是意大利语，德语，或日语都没有赢得这场竞争，而英语成功了。幸运的是，谁输谁赢并不重要。事实上我们要说明

English did. Luckily, this does not mean that there are people who won and people who lost. In fact, we will show that the people whose language seemed to win did not, in fact, improve their positions. The other people won, and those non-native speakers will soon win even more. This is one of the many "Globish Paradoxes."

的是，那些在语言上貌似有优势的人恰似并没有处于有利的地位。虽然英语母语人士赢得了竞争，然而非英语母语人士将会取到更大的优势。这就是众多的"全球语悖论"之一。

Technical

Grammar - the structure of words in a sentence.

Pronounce - to speak accurate sounds in a language

Stress - making a heavy tone on one syllable of a word

Syllable - a part of a word you are saying

Paradox - something that sounds correct but is really the opposite like: *winning is really losing*

Verb - the part of speech that tells the action in a sentence.

International

Pajamas - clothes you wear to bed at night

Chapter 4

The Native English Speakers' Edge is Their Problem

Speaking an extra language is always good. It makes it easier to admit that there are different ways of doing things. It also helps to understand other cultures, to see why they are valued and what they have produced. You can discover a foreign culture through traveling and translation. But truly understanding is another thing: that requires some mastery of its language to talk with people of the culture, and to read their most important books. The "not created here" idea comes from fear and dislike of foreign things and culture. It makes people avoid important ideas and new ways of working.

Native English speakers, of course, speak English most of the time - with their families,

第四章

英语母语人士的优势正是他们的劣势

能够多说一种语言总是有好处的。这使得人们更容易接受做事情有不同的方法。这也有助于了解其他文化，知道为什么他们得到尊重以及他们创造了什么。你可以通过旅行和翻译来了解外国文化。但是要完完全全的了解却是另一回事：那需要精通外语，与生长在这个文化里的人们交流，并阅读其最重要的书籍。"非我所创"这种想法来源于对外来事物及文化的恐惧和厌恶。它会使人们错过重要的想法以及新的工作方式。

当然，英语母语人士大部分时间都在与他们的家人，同事，

the people they work with, their neighbors, and their personal friends. Sometimes they talk to non-native speakers in English, but most English speakers do not do this often. On the other hand, a Portuguese man speaks English most often with non-native English speakers. They all have strange accents. His ears become sympathetic. He learns to listen and understand and not be confused by the accent. He learns to understand a Korean, a Scotsman or a New Zealander with strong local accents. And he learns to understand the pronunciations of others learning English. Often, he understands accents much better than a native English speaker.

It is a general observation that the person who already speaks five languages has very little difficulty learning the sixth one. Even the person who masters two languages is in a much better position to learn a third one

邻居，以及朋友说英语。有时候他们会用英语与非英语母语人士交谈，但并不是经常。而另一方面，一个葡萄牙人却常常用英语同非英语母语人士交流。这些人的发音都很古怪。于是他的耳朵开始适应别人的口音。他学着倾听并理解别人的话，而不被他们的口音所干扰。他学会理解韩国人，苏格兰人，或新西兰人的浓重口音。同时他也学会了理解其他英语学习者的发音。通常，他会比一个英语母语人士更能听懂别人的口音。

一般来说，一个已经会说五种语言的人在学习第六种语言时并不会遇到什么困难。即使是掌握两种语言的人，在学习第三种语言时也要比他的那些只会母语的同胞们处于更有利的地位。这就是为什么很可惜现

than the countryman or countrywoman who sticks only to the mother tongue. That is why it is too bad people no longer speak their local patois. The practice almost disappeared during the 20th century.

在人们都不再说他们的家乡话了。这种习俗在20世纪就消失殆尽了。

Scientists tell us that having a second language seems to enable some mysterious brain connections which are otherwise not used at all. Like muscles with regular exercise, these active connections allow people to learn additional foreign languages more easily.

科学家告诉我们，掌握第二种语言似乎可以激活我们大脑内部之前根本不使用的某种神秘网络。就像经常锻炼的肌肉，这些积极活跃的网络可以使得人们在学习外语时更加轻松。

Now that so many people migrate to English-speaking countries, many of the young people in those families quickly learn English. It is estimated, for example, that 10% of all younger persons in the UK still keep another language after they learn English. Probably similar figures are available in the US. Those children have an extra set of skills when speaking to other new

由于许多人移民到了英语国家，那么这些家庭里的年轻人很快就学会了英语。举例来说，据估算英国10%的年轻人在他们学会英语之后仍然保留着另一语言。这个数字可能与美国的相似。这些孩子在与其他英语初学者交谈时就会拥有额外的技巧。

English language learners.

The British Council is the highest authority on English learning and speaking. It agrees with us in its findings. David Graddol of the British Council is the writer of *English Next*, which is a major study from the British Council. Graddol said (as *translated into Globish*):

> *"(Current findings)… should end any sureness among those people who believe that the global position of English is completely firm and protected. We should not have the feeling that young people of the United Kingdom do not need abilities in additional languages besides English."*

Graddol confirms:

> *"Young people who finish school with only English will face poor job possibilities compared to able*

英国文化协会在英语学习和口语方面是最高权威。他们的调查结果与我们的一致。英国文化协会的大卫·格兰多，也是英国文化协会的重要研究项目《英语走向何方》的作者。格兰多说道（翻译成全球语）：

> *"（目前的研究）…应该使那些确信英语的全球性地位是绝对牢固的人放弃他们的想法了。我们不应该觉得英国的年轻人除了英语之外就不再需要掌握其他语言。"*

格兰多强调：

> *刚刚毕业的年轻人如果只会英语的话，那么与来自其他国家，会说其他语*

young people from other countries who also speak other languages. Global companies and organizations will not want young people who have only English.

Anyone who believes that native speakers of English remain in control of these developments will be very troubled. This book suggests that it is native speakers who, perhaps, should be the most worried. But the fact is that the future development of English is now a global concern and should be troubling us all.

English speakers who have only English may not get very good jobs in a global environment, and barriers preventing them from learning other languages are rising quickly. The

言的出色青年相比将会面临较差的就业机遇。跨国公司和机构将不会愿意雇用只会说英语的年轻人。

那些认为英语母语人士仍然控制着发展方向的人将陷入困境。这本书表明或许英语母语人士最担心的应该是自己。但是事实上，英语未来的发展目前已成为全球关注的问题，而且应该困扰我们所有人。

只会说英语的英语国家人士在全球环境中可能找不到很好的工作，而且阻碍他们学习其他语言的障碍也在迅速

competitive edge (personally, organizationally, and nationally) that English historically provided people who learn it, will go away as English becomes a near-universal basic skill.

English-speaking ability will no longer be a mark of membership in a select, educated, group. Instead, the lack of English now threatens to leave out a minority in most countries rather than the majority of their population, as it was before.

Native speakers were thought to be the "gold standard" (**idioms remain in this section**); as final judges of quality and authority. In the new,

增多。英语在历史上曾经给予那些学习者的竞争优势（个人地，组织上地，以及全国性地）将会随着英语成为普遍性的基本技能而烟消云散。

会说英语不再标志着你属于杰出的，有文化的人群。相反，与以前不同的是，在大多数国家，缺乏英语能力的少数人将面临被忽略的危险，而不是会英语的大多数人。

英语母语人士曾被认为是"黄金标准"（**这一章节仍然保留习语**），是好坏的最终裁判及权

quickly-appearing environment, native speakers may increasingly be indentified as part of the problem rather than being the basic solution. Non-native speakers will feel these "golden" native speakers are bringing along "cultural baggage" of little interest, or as teachers are "gold-plating" the teaching process.

威。在目前这个全新的，日新月异的环境中，英语母语人士可能被越来越多的人视为问题的制造者而不是解决问题的人。非英语母语人士会觉得这些"金贵的"英语母语人士正带来令人不感兴趣的"文化包袱"，或作为老师他们正给教学过程"镀金"。

Traditionally, native speakers of English have been thought of as providing the authoritative standard and as being the best teachers. Now, they may be seen as presenting barriers to the free development of global English.

传统观点认为，英语母语人士可以提供权威的标准并成为最好的教师。但现在，他们被视为正在给英语的全球发展制造障碍。

We are now nearing

英语母语人士凭借

the end of the period where native speakers can shine in their special knowledge of the global "lingua franca."

Now David Graddol is an expert on this subject. But he is also an Englishman. It would be difficult for him - or any native English speaker - to see all that non-native speakers see... and see differently.

For example, non-native speakers see how native English speakers believe that their pronunciation is the only valid one. Pronunciation is not easy in English. There are versions of English with traditional or old colonial accents. Many different British accents were mixed in the past with local languages in colonies such as America, India, South Africa, Hong Kong, Australia, or New Zealand. Today more accents are becoming common as English gets mixed with the

他们所掌握的国际通用语知识辉煌一时，而我们现在正处于这个时代末尾。

如今大卫·格兰多已成为这一学科的专家。但是他也是一位英国人，因此对于他或任何英语母语人士来说，从所有非英语母语人士的相同角度及不同角度看问题是很难的。

举个例子，非英语母语人士注意到英语母语人士坚信他们的发音才是正确的。但英语的发音并不简单。有的英语带有传统口音，有的带有旧殖民地口音。过去有许多不同的英国口音与殖民地的当地口音相混合，例如美国，印度，南非，香港，澳大利亚，或新西兰。如今随着英语与其他语言的相混合，越来越多的口音变得更加常见。英语学习者们往往需

accents from other languages. Learners of English often have to struggle to hear "native" English and then to manage the different accents. Learners often learn English with the older colonial accents or newer accents. Not many people now speak English like the Queen of England.

Also, native speakers often use their local idioms as if they are universal. (Like saying that someone who dies is "biting the dust". How long does it take to explain what these really mean? The modern global citizen does not need language like that.)

Non-native speakers also observe this: that most native speakers believe they are English experts because they can speak English so easily.

要挣扎着倾听"本土"英语，同时还要应付各种不同口音。这些人学习英语时往往都带有旧殖民地的或新的口音。现在已经没有多少人像英国女王那样说英语了。

另外，英语母语人士经常使用习语好像所有人都理解似的。（例如形容某人死了，就说他"咬尘土"。那么要花上多少时间来解释这个习语的意思？现代的世界公民不需要那样的语言。）

非英语母语人士同样注意到：大多数英语母语人士相信自己是英语方面的专家，因为说英语对他们来说轻而易举。

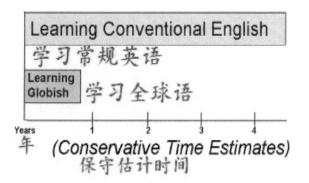

Learning Conventional English
学习常规英语

Learning Globish
学习全球语

Years 年 | 1 | 2 | 3 | 4

(Conservative Time Estimates)
保守估计时间

Language schools in non-English-speaking countries often have native English speakers as teachers. They are said to be the "gold standard" (an *idiom!*) in English.

But these native speakers are not always trained teachers. Often all they have is their ability to pronounce words. They do not know what it is like to learn English. In the end result, a teacher needs to know how to teach.

非英语国家的语言学校常常雇用英语母语人士作为教师。他们被称为英语的"黄金标准"（一个习语）。

但是这些英语母语人士并不全是训练有素的老师。通常他们所拥有的只是单词发音能力。他们并不知道学习英语是什么滋味。总而言之，一个教师需要知道如何教学。

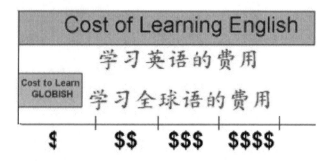

Cost of Learning English
学习英语的费用

Cost to Learn GLOBISH
学习全球语的费用

$ | $$ | $$$ | $$$$

So sometimes non-native English speakers become better teachers of English than people with the perfect UK, or US, or South African English pronunciation.

In the past, English schools have made a lot of money using native speakers to teach English. Thus the students always work towards a goal that is always out of reach. Probably none of these students will ever speak the Queen's English. To achieve that you must be born not far from Oxford or Cambridge. Or, at a minimum, you must have learned English when your voice muscles were still young. That means very early in your life, before 12 years old. Learning to speak without an accent is almost impossible. You will always need more lessons, says the English teacher who wants more work.

But here is the good news: Your accent just needs to be

有时非英语母语人士成为了英语教师，而且要比那些拥有正宗英国，美国，或南非英语发音的人更好。

过去，英语学校通过雇用英语母语人士来教授英语而赚了很多钱。因而学生们总是朝着一个永远也达不到的目标而努力。也许这些学生中没有一个能够说标准英语。想要达到那个目标，你必须生长在距离牛津或剑桥不远的地方。或者，至少在你的发音器官发育成熟之前就已经学习了英语。这意味着在你非常年轻的时候，12岁之前。想要说一口没有口音的英语几乎是不可能的。想要上更多课、赚更多钱的老师说道：你需要不停的学习。

但是告诉你一个好消息：你的

"understandable"...not perfect. Learners of English often need to stop and think about what they are doing. It is wise to remember to ask: how much English do I *need*? Do I need *all* the fine words and perfect pronunciation? Perhaps not....

口音不需要完美，而只需要达到"可以理解的"水平。英语学习者们需要时常停下来思考他们正在做什么。聪明的人总会记得问自己：我*需要*多少英语？我是否真的需要*所有的*华丽辞藻以及完美发音？或许并不需要....

Technical

Idiom - a term for the use of colorful words which may not be understood by non-native speakers.

Lesson - one section of a larger course of study

International

Migrate - to move your home from one country to another. Also: an immigrant is a person who migrates.

Chapter 5

The English Learners' Problem...Can Be Their Edge

Some very expert English speakers take pride in speaking what is called "plain" English. They recommend we use simple English words, and to avoid foreign, borrowed words for example. So speaking plain English is not speaking bad English at all, and might even be speaking rather good English. Using unusual or difficult words does not always mean you know what you are talking about. In many cases, "plain" English is far more useful than other English. The term "Plain English" is the name of a small movement, but the term is most often used between native speakers to tell each other that the subject is too difficult. They say: *"Just tell me in plain English!"*

第五章

英语学习者的劣势... 可以是他们的优势

一些非常专业的英语人士对他们可以说所谓的"简明"英语而感到自豪。他们建议我们使用简单的英语词汇，例如避免使用外来词语。所以，说简明英语并不意味着你的英语很差，甚至有可能是说好的英语。使用不常见的或难以理解的词语并不总是意味着你知道自己在说什么。在很多情况下，"简明"英语比其他英语要更加有用。"简明英语"最初是一个规模不大的运动组织的名称，但是这个词大多在英语母语人士告诉对方他们谈论的话题太难理解的时候使用。他们说：

"用简单明了的英语告诉我就

行啦！"

It is very important, on the other hand, to speak correct English. Correct English means using common English words in sentences that have reasonably good meanings. Of course, everyone makes mistakes now and then, but a good goal is to say things in a correct way using simple words. This makes it easier to say things that are useful.

Of course, we know that we say things well enough if people understand what we say. So we need to observe a level of usage and correctness in English which is "enough" for understanding. Less is not enough. And "more than enough" is too much - too difficult - for many people to understand. Most public messages - such as advertisements use fairly common words and fairly simple English. The messages often cost a lot so it is important everyone understands them. On

而另一方面，说正确的英语也非常重要。正确的英语就是在句子中使用常见的英语单词表达恰当的意思。当然，每个人都会时常犯错，但是以正确的方法及简单的词语来述说事情正是我们美好的目标。这会使得描述实际价值的事情更加轻松。

毫无疑问，如果人们理解我们所说的那就证明我们描述的很好。所以我们需要注意观察正确使用英语达到何种水平就可以"足够"让人理解。低于这个水平是不够的，而"绰绰有余"又太多了——因为很多人理解不了。大多数公共信息——例如广告，使用极其普通的词汇和相当简单的英语。发布这样的信息往往需要花费很多钱，因此重要的是要让每个人都理解。在电视上播放广告非常昂

46

television, time for messages can cost huge amounts so the English used is chosen very carefully. The American Football Super Bowl in the US has advertisements that are very easy to understand. The advertisers pay $2 000 000 a minute for their advertisements, so they want to be sure people understand!

There is a level of English that is acceptable for most purposes of understanding. This is the level that Globish aims to show. As we will see in greater detail, Globish is a defined subset of English. Because it is limited, everyone can learn the same English words and then they can understand each other. Globish uses simple sentence structures and a small number of words, so that means you have to learn less. And it can be expanded easily when people choose to do this.

The Globish word list has 1500 words. They have been carefully chosen from all the

贵，所以使用的英语词汇需要精心挑选。在美国超级碗美式足球冠军赛期间播放的广告都非常容易理解。广告商们需要每分钟支付两百万美元播放他们的广告，因此他们要确保人们理解他们的广告词。

这样的英语就达到了可以令大多数人理解的水平。全球语的目的就是要展示这样的英语。而我们之后会详细看到的就是全球语是一个轮廓分明的英语子集。因为它是有限的，所以每个人都学习同样的英语词汇，这样他们就可以理解对方。全球语使用简单的句子结构以及少量的词汇，也就是说你需要学习的量很少。而当人们选择这样做之后也很容易扩展。

全球语的词汇表中含有 1500 个单词。它们是作者从所有最

most common words in English. They are listed in the middle of this book. In the Oxford English Dictionary there are about 615000 entries. So how could 1500 words be enough? This book – in Globish – uses those 1500 basic words and their variations.

This list of 1500, of course, will also accept a few other words which are tied to a trade or an industry: call them "technical words." (Technical is a technical word.) Some technical words are understood everywhere. In the computer industry, words like web and software are usually known by everyone. They are from English or are made up, like Google. And in the cooking industry, many words are French, like "sauté" or "omelette".

Globish also uses words that are already international. Travelers communicate using words like "pizza", "hotel",

常用的英语单词中精心挑选出来的。词汇表位于这本书的中间位置。《牛津英语大词典》中收录了大约 615000 个词条，那么 1500 个单词怎么能够用呢？《全球语》这本书就是用这 1500 个单词及其变体写成的。

当然，这 1500 个单词的词汇表会包含一些与贸易或工业相关联的词汇：我们称之为"专业术语"。（专业的就是一个专业术语。）有些专业术语所有人都明白。在计算机产业中，通常每个人都知道例如网络和软件这样的词。这些词有的来自英语，有的是编造出来的，例如 Google(谷歌)。在烹饪行业，有许多法语词汇，像"煎炒"或"煎蛋卷"。

全球语同时也使用那些已经国际化的词语。旅行者们交流时使用的词语，例如"pizza(比

"police", "taxi", "stop", "restaurant", "toilets", and "photo".

萨)", "hotel(宾馆)", "police(警察)", "taxi(出租车)", "stop(车站)", "restaurant(餐厅)", "toilets(厕所)", 和"photo(照片)"。

1500 is a lot of words, because English has been a language where words "father" words. The children words of the first 1500 words are easy to learn. For instance, "care" is the father of "careful, carefully, carefulness, careless, carelessly, carelessness, uncaring, caretaker, etc..." It is the same with "use" and hundreds of other words. If you count all the fathers and their children you find over 5,000 Globish words.

1500 个单词的量很大，因为英语是一种词"生"词的语言。1500 个基本词汇衍生出来的词语是很容易掌握的。例如，"careful(仔细的), carefully(小心地), carefulness(仔细), careless(粗心的), carelessly(粗心地), carelessness(粗心大意), uncaring(冷漠的), caretaker(管理员/看门人),等等..."就来自于"care(关心)"。"use(使用)"和其他几百个词汇亦是如此。如果你将基本词汇和它们的衍生词都计算在内，那么全球语的词汇量将超过 5000 个。

Experts say most native English speakers use only about 3,500 words. Well-

专家认为大多数英语母语人士仅仅使用大约 3500 个单词。

educated speakers may know many more words but probably only use about 7,500 words. It is demonstrated that even native speakers with high education say 80% of what they have to say with only 20% of their word-wealth. This is only one good example of a universal law called the "Pareto Principle", named after its Paris-born inventor. The Pareto Principle states: For all things that happen, 80% of the results come from 20% of the causes. So, 20% of the educated native speaker's 7500 word wealth is….1500. So with 1500 words, you may communicate better than the average native English speaker, and perhaps as well as the highly-educated one – for 80% of the ideas. For the 20% left over, in Globish you can use a definition instead. You will not say "my nephew", as this could be too difficult in many non-English speaking countries. You will say instead: "the son of my

受过良好教育的人可能掌握更多的词汇，但很可能只使用7500个左右的单词。研究证明，即使是拥有高学历的英语母语人士也只是使用他们20%的词汇量就可以表达他们80%的思想。这是普遍规律"帕雷托法则"的一个很好的例子，这个法则是以在巴黎出生的创造者的名字命名的。帕雷托法则规定：对于发生的每件事情，80%的结果取决于20%的原因。那么受过教育的英语母语人士所掌握的7500个词汇的20%就是…1500个。因此，如果用这1500个词来表达80%的想法，你可以比一般的英语母语人士更好地与人交流，或许会与受过高等教育的人差不多。对于剩下的20%，你完全可以用全球语进行解释。你将不会说"我的侄子"，因为对于非英语母语人士来说这有可能太难了，你可以改口

brother". It will be all right.

说："我兄弟的儿子"。这样就行了。

But where did the 1500 words come from?

但是这 1500 个单词是从哪里来的呢？

Various lists of most-commonly-used English words have suggested the 1500 basic words of Globish. However, the value of a set of words should not be by the place they come from but how well we use them.

全球语的 1500 个基本词汇是从许多最常用的英语词汇表中挑选出来的。无论如何，一组单词的价值并不应该在于它们的出处，而是在于我们如何使用它们。

Globish is correct English *and* it can communicate with the greatest number of people all over the world. Of course, native English speakers can understand it very quickly because it is English. And even better: they usually do not notice that it is Globish. But non-native English speakers *do* see the difference: they understand the Globish better than the English they usually hear from native English speakers.

全球语是正确的英语而且用它可以与世界上的大部分人进行交流。当然，英语母语人士可以很快的理解因为这就是英语。而更好的是：他们通常不会注意到你说的就是全球语。但是非英语母语人士肯定能注意到不同：比起英语母语人士通常说的英语，他们对全球语的理解要更好。

Technical Words

Technical - with a scientific basis, or used by a profession

International Words

Pizza - an Italian food found most places in the world

Hotel - a place to stay which rents many rooms by the night

Police - men or women who make certain you follow the law.

Taxi - a car and driver you rent to take you individual places

Restaurant - a place to eat where you buy single meals

Toilets - places to wash hands and do other necessary things

Photo - a picture taken with a camera

Piano - a large box with many keys to make music with

Sauté - French way of cooking; makes meat or vegetables soft

Omelette - a way of cooking meals with eggs

Chapter 6
The Value of a Middle Ground

There is a story about one of the authors. He worked for an American oil exploration company in his youth. He did not grow up in Oklahoma or Texas like the other workers. One time he had to work with map makers in the high plains of Wyoming. There, the strong winds are always the enemy of communication.

His job was to place recording devices on a long line with the map makers. He would go ahead first with a tall stick, and the oil company map makers behind would sight the stick from far away. They waved at him, to guide him left or right. Then he would shout out the number of the device he planted there, on that straight line. The wind was very loud and he had to shout over it.

第六章
中间地带的价值

这里有个关于一个作家的故事。他年轻的时候为美国的一家石油勘探公司工作。他的同事们都是在俄克拉荷马州或德克萨斯州长大的，而他却不是。一次，他不得不与地图绘制人员在怀俄明州的高原上工作。在那里，强风总是阻碍人们的交流。

他的工作是与地图绘制人员一起沿着一条长线放置记录设备。他会拿着一根长长的杆子走在前面，而石油公司的地图绘制人员会在后面很远的地方用仪器观察。他们会朝他挥手，引导他向左或向右。之后他要大声喊出沿着那条直线放置的设备数量。狂风呼啸着，而他的音量必须盖过风的声

But often the map makers from Oklahoma and Texas would just shake their heads. They could not understand what he shouted. The boy couldn't talk right - they said.

Then one night, all the men had drinks together. They said they did not want to fire him, but they could not understand his numbers in the wind. After a few more drinks, they decided they could be language teachers. They taught him a new way to count, so the wind would not take away the numbers when he shouted them.

Some of the numbers in the new dialect of English sounded familiar, but others were totally different: (1) "wuhn" (2) "teu" (3) "thray" (4) "foar" (5) "fahve" (6) "seex" (7) "sebn" (8) "ate" (9) "nahne" (10) "teeyuhn" (11) "lebn", and on like that. The map-makers were very happy, and not just because of the drinks. They had saved more than a job. They felt

音。但是这些来自俄克拉荷马和德克萨斯的地图绘制人员往往只是冲着他摇头。他们听不懂他喊了什么。这孩子不会说话——他们说道。

后来，一天晚上所有人在一起喝酒。地图绘制人员说他们不想解雇他，但是他们听不懂他在刮风时喊的数字。酒过数巡之后，他们决定当一回语言老师。他们教他一种新的计数方法，这样即使是刮大风的时候，他们也可以听清楚他喊的数字。

有些数字在这新的英语方言中听起来很熟悉，但是其他的却完全不同：(1) "wuhn" (一) (2) "teu" (二) (3) "thray" (三) (4) "foar" (四) (5) "fahve" (五) (6) "seex" (六) (7) "sebn" (七) (8) "ate" (八) (9) "nahne" (九) (10)

they had saved a soul. They had taught someone to "talk right" as they knew it.

Many people have experiences like this. If we do not speak different languages or dialects, at least we speak differently at times. We can copy different accents. Sometimes we speak in new ways to make it easier for others to understand us, and sometimes to sound like others so we are more like them. We often use different ways of speaking for jokes.

It should be easy to use Globish - the same words for everyone everywhere in the world. One language for everyone would be the best tool ever. It would be a tool for communication in a

"teeyuhn"（十）(11) "lebn"（十一），这样依此类推。这些地图绘制人员非常开心，但不只是因为喝酒。他们挽救的不仅是一份工作，他们觉得他们还挽救了一个灵魂。他们教会了某人用他们熟知的方式来"正常说话"。

许多人都曾有那样的经历。如果我们不会说不同的语言或方言，至少我们偶尔会转换说话的方式。我们可以模仿不同的口音。有时，我们用不同的方式说话是为了让其他人能够更容易理解，而有时我们模仿别人这样我们就可以更相像。通常我们会用不同的说话方式来讲笑话。

全球语应该易于使用——因为世界上任何地方的任何人都会使用同样的词语。一种所有人都使用的语言将永远是最好的语言。它将成为一种有用的交

useful way. It might not be as good for word games as English, or as good for describing deep feelings. But Globish would be much better for communication between – or with – people who are not native English speakers. And, of course, native English speakers could understand it too.

So Globish makes an effective tool. You'll be able to do almost anything with it, with a good understanding of what it is and how it works.

But Globish does not aim to be more than a tool, and that is why it is different from English. English is a cultural language. It is a very rich language. It sometimes has 20 different words to say the same thing. And it has a lot of different ways of using them in long, *long* sentences. Learning all the rest of English is a lifetime of work but there is a good reward. People who learn a lot of English have a rich world of culture to explore. They do a

流工具。它可能不会像英语那样可以玩拼字游戏，或许也不能用来表达深厚的感情。但全球语将是非英语母语人士之间或与非英语母语人士进行交流的更好工具。当然，英语母语人士也能理解。

所以全球语是个有效的工具。只要你很好的理解了它是什么以及它的原理，那么你几乎可以用它做任何事情。

但是全球语的目标仅仅是作为一个工具，而这就是它与英语的不同之处。英语是一门文化语言。它是一门非常丰富的语言。有时英语中可以用 20 个不同的词来说同样的事物。而且英语很长很长的句子中还有很多不同的用词方法。要学会全部的英语是一项需要倾注一生的工作，但也会有丰厚的回报。学习了很多英语知识的人

lot of learning and can do a lot with what they learn.

But Globish does not aim so high. It is just meant to be a necessary amount. Globish speakers will enjoy travel more, and can do business in Istanbul, Kiev, Madrid, Seoul, San Francisco and Edinburgh.

This will be worth repeating: *Globish is "enough" and less than Globish would be not enough. But more than Globish could be too much, and when you use too much English, many people will not understand you.*

This confuses some people, especially English teachers. They say: "How is better English, richer English, *not always* better?" English teachers like people to enjoy the language, to learn more and more English. It is their

们都有一个丰富的文化世界可供探索。他们有很多东西学习而且可以用他们所学的知识做很多事情。

但是全球语的目标并没有那么高。它注定了只要够用就好。说全球语的人将会喜欢更多的旅行，而且可以在伊斯坦布尔，基辅，马德里，首尔，旧金山，及爱丁堡这些地方做生意。

有必要重申的是：*全球语是"足够的"，低于全球语的水平将是不够的。但是高于全球语的水平又可能太多了，而且当你说过多的英语时，很多人将不能理解你的意思。*

这使一些人感到困惑，特别是英语教师们。他们说："更好的英语，更丰富的英语，怎么就不一定好呢？"英语教师希望人们喜欢英语，学习越来越多的英语知识。这是他们的工

job.

When we see native speakers speak English it seems so easy. We think it should be easy for non-native speakers too. But when we look at English tests, we see that all kinds of English are used. There is no clear level of English, just more and more of it. For example, the TOEIC (Test of English for International Communication) does not tell you when you are ready. It does not say when you have "acceptable" English. Globish is a standard that you can reach. A Globish test can tell you if you have a required amount of language to communicate with other people. That is what brings "understanding" – and either we have it, or we don't.

The British Council says (in Globish again):

"For ELF (English as

作。

当英语母语人士说英语时，在我们看来这太简单了。因此我们以为对于非英语母语人士来说也应该很简单。但是当我们留意英语考试的时候，就会发现有各种各样的英语。只有越来越多的英语考试，却没有一个清晰地标准。举个例子，托业考试（国际交流英语测评）并不会体现出你是否已达到标准。通过参加托业考试你并不会知道你是否已拥有"可以接受的"英语水平。而全球语却是一个你可以达到的标准。完成全球语的测试你就可以知道你是否已达到与他人交流所需要的语言水平。正是语言促进了"理解"——要么我们达到了水平，要么就没有。

英国文化协会声明：（再次译成全球语）

"使用 ELF（英语通

a Lingua Franca) being _understood_ is most important, rather more important than being perfect. The goal of English – within the ELF idea – is not a native speaker but a good speaker of two languages, with a national accent and some the special skills to achieve understanding with another non-native speaker."

用语）让人_理解_是最重要的，比做到完美更加重要。在ELF的设想中，英语的目标并不是英语母语人士，而是一个能说好两种语言，带有本国的口音并运用一些特殊技巧从而使另一个非英语母语人士能够理解他的人。"

These non-native speakers, in many cases, speak much less perfect English than native speakers. Speaking with words that go past the words they understand is the best way to lose them. It is better then, to stay within the Globish borders. It is better to do that than to act as if you believe that the best English shows the highest social status. **With Globish, we are all from the same world.**

在很多情况下，这些非英语母语人士说的英语没有英语母语人士说的好。如果你使用超过他们理解能力的词汇，那么他们肯定无法理解你的意思。如果你使用的是全球语的词汇，效果就会更好。这样做的话要比你假装相信一流的英语代表最高的社会地位要好得多。**有了全球语，我们都来自同一个世界。**

Chapter 7
The Beginnings of Globish

The *most* important thing about Globish is that it started with non-native English speakers. Some English professor could have said "I will now create Globish to make English easy for these adults who are really children." Then Globish would not be global, but just some English professor's plaything. But the true Globish idea started in international meetings with British, Americans, continental Europeans, and Japanese, and then Koreans. The communication was close to excellent between the British and the Americans. But it was not good between those two and the other people. Then there was a big surprise: the communication

第七章
全球语的开端

全球语*最*重要的一点是，它是从非英语母语人士开始的。某个英语教授本来可以说道："现在我将要创造全球语以使那些英语只有儿童水平的成年人学起来更轻松。"那么全球语将只会成为某个英语教授的玩物而不会成为全球性的了。但是全球语真正的想法是从与英国人，美国人，欧洲大陆人，日本人，以及韩国人之间的国际会议中萌发的。英国人与美国人之间的交流近乎完美。但是这两个国家的人与其他国家的人交流却不是很好。之后令人称奇的是：最后三组人，欧洲大陆人，日本人，和韩国人之间的交流是最好的。这似乎有个好的理由：他们之

between the last three groups, continental Europeans, Japanese, and Koreans, was among the best. There seemed to be one good reason: they were saying things with each other that they would have been afraid to try with the native English speakers – for fear of losing respect. So all of these non-native speakers felt comfortable and safe in what sounded like English, but was far from it.

But those non-native English speakers were all *talking* to each other. Yes, there were many mistakes. And yes, the pronunciation was strange. The words were used in unusual ways. Many native English speakers think English like this is horrible. However, the non-native speakers were enjoying their communication.

But as soon as one of the English or Americans started

间说的话是那些他们不敢尝试与英语母语人士说的，因为他们害怕说了之后会失去别人对他们的尊重。因此所有这些非英语母语人士都觉得用这听起来像英语的英语交谈很舒服和安全，但他们使用的却远远不是英语。

但是这些非英语母语人士全都在相互*交谈*。确实，他们的语言中有很多错误。当然，他们的发音很怪。词语的使用方法也不寻常。许多英语母语人士认为这样的英语太糟糕了。然而，非英语母语人士却享受着这样的交流。

但是一旦其中的一个英国人或

speaking, everything changed in one second. The non-native speakers stopped talking; most were afraid of speaking to the native English speakers. None of them wanted to say a word that was incorrect.

It is often that way across the world. Non-native English speakers have many problems with English. Some native English speakers say non-natives speak "broken English." In truth, non-native English speakers talk to each other effectively *because* they respect and share the same limitations.

The Frenchman and the Korean know they have similar limitations. They do not use rare, difficult-to-understand English words. They choose words that are "acceptable" because they are the easiest words they both know. Of course, these are not always those of the native speakers, who have so many more words to choose from.

美国人开始说话，一切马上都改变了。非英语母语人士停止了交谈；大多数人害怕与英语母语人士说话。他们当中没有人愿意说一个错误的词。

这种情况在世界各地时常发生。非英语母语人士的英语有很多问题。一些英语母语人士说非英语母语人士讲的是"蹩脚英语"。事实上，非英语母语人士之间的谈话效率很高是因为他们尊重并分担共同的局限。

法国人和韩国人清楚他们有相似的局限。他们不会使用不常见的，难以理解的英语词汇。他们选择"可接受的"词语是因为这些是双方都知晓的最简单的词汇。当然，对于英语母语人士来说不总是这样，他们有更多的词汇可以选择。

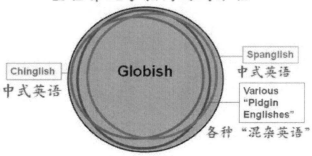

Nearly-Identical Limitations Worldwide
全世界几乎相同的局限性

Chinglish
中式英语

Globish

Spanglish
中式英语

Various
"Pidgin
Englishes"

各种"混杂英语"

Globish Combines Limitations
全球语同局限性相结合

The idea of Globish came from this observation: limitations are not always a problem. In fact, they can be useful, if you understand them. Jean-Paul Nerrière could see that *"if we can make the limitations exactly the same, it will be as if there are no limitations at all"*. He decided to record a limited set of words and language that he observed in most non-English speakers. He then suggested that people from various mother tongues can communicate better if they use these carefully chosen limitations. Globish is that "common ground."

全球语的想法来自以下这一观察：局限并不一定就是麻烦。事实上，如果你理解了他们，它们也可以利用的。让-保罗·内里埃能够看出："如果我们能让每个人的局限都完全相同，那么每个人就如同根本没有局限一样。"他决定记录下观察到的大多数非英语母语人士使用的一组数量有限的词汇和语言。之后他表示，如果不同母语的人使用这些精心挑选的词汇，那么他们之间的交流会更顺畅。全球语就是那个"共同基础"。

This theory of limitations is not as strange as it might seem at first. Most human activities have some limitations.

The World Cup is one of the most-watched competitions in the world, because its set of "limitations" makes it a great game for everyone. In this game of foot-ball, players must use their feet most of the time to control the ball, so tall people and people with big arms do not always win. Some people say it is dancing with the ball; the limitations make it beautiful.

Ballet, of course, has limitations too; it is what you say with your body. And people of every language enjoy both of these. The beauty happens when the limitations are the same. Globish is about having the same limitations, so there is no limit to what can be communicated between people speaking or writing or reading Globish.

这个局限理论并不像它起初那样奇怪。大多数人类活动都有某种规则。

世界杯是世界上收视率最高的比赛之一，那是因为它的一套"规则"让它成为每个人都喜爱的运动。在足球这种比赛中，运动员大多数时间内必须使用他们的脚来控制球，因此高大以及上身强壮的人并不一定会赢。有些人说这是与球共舞；它的规则使其变得优美。

当然，芭蕾舞也有规则；那就是用身体语言进行表达。尽管世界上的人说不同的语言，但他们都喜欢足球和芭蕾。当规则相同时，人们就感到了美的存在。全球语就是为了让人们拥有共同的局限，那样的话，在使用全球语交谈、写作或阅读的时候，就没有什么可以妨

We hope the dancers will not start singing in ballets. But what happens when you can use your hands in "football?" Then – mostly in the English-speaking cultures – we see their American football and Rugby football. These do not have the limitations of playing only with their feet. Not as many people in the world can sit together and enjoy watching. It is not something they all can share, all knowing the same limitations.

The limitations of Globish also make it easier to learn, easier to find a word to use. Native English speakers seem to have too many words that say the same thing and too many ways to say it.

So communication between non-native speakers can be much more effective when they are using Globish. And if non-native and native speakers use Globish between themselves, both of

碍人们的交流了。

我们期望芭蕾舞演员们不会开始在舞蹈中歌唱。但当你在"足球"比赛中使用手时会发生什么呢？于是，我们注意到在大多数英语国家有美式足球和橄榄球。这些运动没有规定只能用脚进行比赛。因此世界上没有那么多人能够坐在一起欣赏。这不是他们每个人都可以分享的，也不是每个人都了解同样的规则。

全球语的局限也使得它更容易学习，更容易找到要使用的词语。英语母语人士似乎有太多的词汇及太多的方法来表达同样的意思。

因此当非英语母语人士都使用全球语时，他们之间的交流可以更有效率。而且如果非英语母语人士与英语母语人士使用全球语互相交流的话，双方都

them will understand. Most people would think that native English speakers could know how to speak Globish in one second. But that is not true. Native English speakers who use too many words in too many ways are, in fact, missing a huge opportunity to communicate with the world.

The British Council tells us (here in Globish):

"People have wondered for years whether English is so solid in international communication that even the rise of China could not move it from its high position. The answer is that there is already a new language, which was being spoken quietly while native-speakers of English were looking the other way. These native-speakers of English were too happy when they thought their

可以理解。多数人认为英语母语人士瞬间就能学会如何说全球语，但这并不是事实。实际上，因为使用太多的词汇及太多的表达方式，英语母语人士正错过一个与世界交流的大好良机。

英国文化协会告诉我们（这里用全球语说）：

"这些年来人们都好奇英语在国际交流中的地位是如此牢固，以至于甚至是中国的崛起都没能够动摇它的领导地位。答案是正当英语母语人士视而不见的时候，人们已经静静地使用一种新的语言了。当想到他们的语言是最好的时候，这些英

language was the best of all. The new language that is pushing out the language of Shakespeare as the world's Lingua Franca is English itself – English in its new global form. As this book (English Next) shows, this is not English as we have known it, and have taught it in the past as a foreign language. It is a new happening, and if it represents any kind of winning, it will probably not be the cause of celebration by native English speakers."

语母语人士太过高兴了。那个将莎士比亚的语言排挤出去而成为世界通用语的新语言正是英语自身——全新的英语全球性形式。正如这本书（《英语走向何方》）所说明的，这样的英语不是我们所熟知的英语，也不是过去我们当作外语进行教授的英语。这是一件新的东西，即使这代表着任何形式的胜利，它也不太可能是由英语母语人士的沾沾自喜带来的。"

The British Council continues (in our Globish):

英国文化协会继续说道（用我们的全球语）：

"In organizations where English has

"在那些英语已成为

68

become the business language, meetings sometimes go more smoothly when no native speakers are present. Globally, the same kind of thing may be happening, on a larger scale. This is not just because non-native speakers fear to talk to a native speaker. The change is that soon the problem may be that few native speakers will be accepted in the community of lingua franca users. The presence of native English speakers gets in the way of communication."

商业用语的组织机构中，当没有英语母语人士出席的时候，有时会议反而会进行的更加流畅。就全球范围来说，这种现象可能大规模的存在。这并不仅仅是因为非英语母语人士害怕与英语母语人士交谈。问题的转变在于很快可能只有很少的英语母语人士会被通用语使用者群体所接纳。英语母语人士的存在恰恰阻碍了交流。"

Strangely, many native English speakers still believe they can do all things better than non-native speakers just because they speak better English. How long will it take for them to understand that they are wrong? They have a

奇怪的是，很多英语母语人士仍然相信他们事事都可以做的比非英语母语人士好，只是因为他们的英语说得更好。到底需要多长时间他们才能明白他

problem that *they are not able to understand.* They do not see that many non-native speakers simply cannot understand them. This does not mean the native speaker's English is bad. It means that their *communication* is bad; sometimes they do not even attempt to make their communication useful to everyone. Often they don't know how.

We want everyone to be able to speak to and understand everyone. There is a middle ground, but the native English speakers are not the ones drawing the borders. And because you may not be able to say this to a native speaker, who might not be able to understand – we will say it here.

To belong to the international community, a native English speaker must:

- **understand....** what is explained in this book,

- **accept....** that it is the fact of a new world which has

们是错的？他们的问题是他们不能够理解他人。他们没有注意到许多非英语母语人士完全听不懂他们说什么。这并不意味着这些英语母语人士的英语不好。而是他们的沟通能力太差；有时他们甚至都不愿去尝试使每个人都从沟通中受益。往往他们不知道该怎么样做。

我们希望每个人都可以互相交谈并理解对方。人们之间有个中间地带，但是这界限不是由英语母语人士来划分的。由于你可能无法将这一点告诉一个英语母语人士，因为他或许不能理解你说的话——我们会在这里说明。

想要成为国际社会的一员，一个英语母语人士必须做到：

- **理解**....正如这本书中解释的，

- **接受**...事实就是新的世界

many new powers that will be as strong as the English-speaking countries,

- decide **to change** with this new reality, in order to still be a member.

Whenever a native English speaker acts as if *you* are the stupid one, **please give them this book**. If they choose to take no notice of their problem, they will be left out of communication. They will be left out of activities with others – worldwide – if they do not learn to "limit" the way they use their language. English speakers need to limit both spoken and written English for communication with non-native English speakers. In short, they too need to "learn" Globish. It is not an easy exercise, but it can be done. Some of this book will help them.

Globish has a special name

It is very important that the

格局中许多新兴强国将会与英语国家一样强大，

- 为了继续成为其中的一员，下决心与新的现实情况一同**改变**。

如果你遇到一个在行为上认为你愚蠢的英语母语人士，那么无论什么时候**请将这本书给他们**。如果他们选择对他们的问题不予理睬，那么他们将会被忽视。如果他们不去学习如何"限制"使用他们的说话方式，那么他们将会在世界范围内被其他人所冷落。在与非英语母语人士交流时，英语母语人士需要在口语和书面语方面都进行限制。简言之，他们也需要"学习"全球语。这不是件容易的事，但是可以做到。这本书中的一些内容将会帮助他们。

全球语有个特殊的名字

全球语的名字不是"全世界的

Globish name is *not* "English for the World" or even "Simple English." If its name were *any kind* of English, the native English speakers would say. "OK, we won. Now all you have to do is speak better English." Without the name Globish, they will not understand it is a special kind of English, and it is no longer "their" English. Most native English speakers who understand this should decide they like it. Hopefully they will say: "Now I understand that I am very lucky. Now my language will be changed a little for the rest of the world. Let me do my best, and they can do their best, and we will meet in the middle."

So *Globish* is a word that tells native English speakers – and non-native speakers – that Globish has a different meaning. Globish is the global language, the language people everywhere

英语"或者甚至"简单英语"，这一点非常重要。如果它的名字是任何形式的英语，那么英语母语人士就会说："好的，我们赢了。你们现在所要做的就是说更好的英语。"如果不叫全球语，那么他们就不会明白这是一种特殊的英语，而且这不再是"他们的"英语。大多数理解这一点的英语母语人士应该决定他们喜欢全球语。但愿他们会说："现在我明白我是幸运的。我的语言现在将为了世界上的其他人而改变一点点。我会尽我所能，他们也会尽其所能，那么我们就会在中间会和。"

因此，全球语这个词告诉英语母语人士和非英语母语人士，全球语具有不同的意义。全球语是全世界的语言，是世界各地的人们都可以使用的语言。全球语这个名字告诉人们，每

can speak. Globish is a name to say that there are limits which everyone can learn. There is a clear set of things they need to learn. And when they learn them, they are done.

Language is equal on this Globish middle ground. No one has an edge. No one can be above anyone else because of language. This is the land where everybody can offer the best ideas with all of his or her professional and personal abilities. Globish will be a foreign language to everyone, without exception. It is not "broken English." It is another version of English to which no native English speaker was born.

We all come together here.

个人都可以学习有限度的东西。他们需要学习的是一套清晰可见的东西。而且当他们掌握了这些东西之后，他们的知识就够用了。

在全球语这个中间地带，语言是平等的。任何人都没有优势。没人能因为语言而高人一等。在这里，每个人都可以凭借自身所有的专业和个人能力提出最好的想法。全球语将无一例外的成为所有人的外语。它不是"蹩脚英语"，它是另一个版本的英语，而且没有一个英语母语人士生来就会。

我们共同来到这里。

Chapter 8
Is Globish More Useful than English?

We talk a lot about international communication, but Globish is also important for *national* communication. In many countries, people speak several languages that are all important. Swiss people speak German, Italian, French or Romansh. Belgians speak French, German, Dutch or Flemish. The largest countries like India, and Russia, and China each have many local languages. Israelis speak Hebrew or Arabic. In many cases, all those people only know their own language. They cannot communicate together because they know only one language; their own. In some countries, even people who *can* speak

第八章
全球语比英语更有用吗？

关于国际交流，我们谈了很多，但是全球语对于国内交流也很重要。在许多国家，人们说数种同等重要的语言。瑞士人说德语，意大利语，法语或罗曼什语。比利时人说法语，德语，荷兰语或佛兰芒语。世界上最大的国家，例如印度，俄罗斯，和中国，每个国家都有很多方言。以色列人说希伯来语或阿拉伯语。在很多情况下，这些人只知道他们自己的语言。他们不能在一起交流是因为他们只会说一种语言，他们自己的语言。在一些国家，能够说其他语言的人们甚至避免使用其他的语言。因为他们

another language try *not* to speak it. It is the language of a group they do not like.

不喜欢的是说那种语言的人。

In all those cases, Globish is the solution. It is much better defined than the "broken English" which is left over from sad school days. Already, in many of these countries, people try to communicate in English just because it is neutral. It is not the language of any one group. Globish is good for them because it offers a solution and is easy to learn.

在所有这些事例中，全球语可以作为解决方案。它比那忧郁的学生时代所剩下的"蹩脚英语"更易学实用。正因为英语是中立的，所以在很多这样的国家中，已经有人尝试用其交流了。这样的语言并不属于任何一部分人。全球语对他们来说很好，因为它提供了一个解决方案并且容易学习。

For people who do not have the time or the money for a full English program, Globish is good. Its plain and simple English will work for them. With Globish they can learn what they need – but no more. They also like the idea of Globish because it is a solution for the person in the street. English, in most cases, is available for educated people, the upper class. In these countries with more than one language, the rich

对于那些没有时间或金钱来学习一整套英语课程的人来说，全球语是件好事。其简单明了的英语对他们很有用。他们可以学习他们所需要的全球语——但不会过多。他们也喜欢全球语的理念，因为它可以为普通人提供解决方案。大多数情况下，有教养的，上流社会的人才有机会学习英语。在那些有多种语言的国家，有钱人可

can travel, and the rich can send their children to study in English-speaking countries. The poorest people also need English, to get ahead in their nation and the world, but they do not have the same resources. Globish will allow the people inside nations to talk more, and do more business there and with the rest of the world. That is the result of Globish - more national talk and more global talk.

What makes Globish more inviting is that people can use it very soon. The learners quickly learn some Globish, then more, then most of what they need, and finally all of it. So, Fast Early Progress (FEP) and a Clear End Point (CEP) improve the student's wish to continue. The Return On Effort (ROE) is just as important as ROI (Return On Investment) is for a business person. In fact, they are very much alike.

以旅行，并且将他们的孩子送到英语国家读书学习。要想在他们的国家或世界上取得成功，贫穷的人们也需要英语，但是他们没有相同的资源。全球语可以让人们在国内更多的进行交流，并与国内的以及世界上其他国家的人们做更多的生意。这就是全球语的成果——更多的国内以及国际交流。

全球语更吸引人的地方在于人们很快就可以使用它。初学者们很快的学习一些全球语，之后更多，接着是他们需要的大部分，最后是全部。因此初期快速进步（FEP）和明确最终目标（CEP）能够增强学生继续学习的渴望。为商务人士预备的付出回报（ROE）与投资回报（ROI）同等重要。事实上，它们很相似。

globish

Fast Early Progress (FEP)	+	Clear End Point (CEP)	=	Return On Effort (ROE)
Build on English you have. Globish doesn't need all the kitchen tools. English measures, cultural ideas, or perfect Oxford Pronunciation		*"Enough English" means you can do the most business, travel in the most countries, and talk to the most people, and write to the most people.*		*From "Enough" - each 5% "better" English requires another year of study. All people don't have the time or the money to be more perfect.*
以你原有的英语为基础。学习全球语并不需要掌握所有的厨房用具，英式计量法，文化观念，或是完美的牛津式发音。		"足够的英语"意思是你可以与大多数人做生意，在大多数国家旅行，并且能与大多数人交谈，给大多数人写信。		从"足够"开始，你的英语每提高5%就需要再学习一年时间，并不是所有的人都会有时间或金钱使自己的英语更完善。

An investor wants to see a valuable return, and a pathway to get there, and a defined end point. In this case, however, every person can be an investor in his or her own future.

The average person in the street has valuable skills or ideas that are not being used. If they cannot operate in all of their nation or all of the world, then those skills or ideas have much less value. So we are all investors.

一个投资者希望看到有价值的回报，一条通向成功的道路，以及一个清晰的目标。那么，在这种情况下，每个人都可以成为自己未来的投资者。

即使是普通人也拥有没有使用的宝贵技能或想法。如果他们不能在他们的国家或全世界施展拳脚，那么这些技能或想法就没有什么价值了。所以我们都是投资者。

There are several ways to learn Globish. Some learners know about 350 to 500 common words in English and can read and say them. Learning Globish can take these people about 6 months if they study for an hour every day, including practice writing and speaking. In six months, with more than 120 days of learning, they can learn just 10 words a day. That should not be too hard.

There may not be a class in Globish near you. However, if you know the limitations given in this book, you can direct a local English teacher to give you only those Globish words and only those Globish sentence structures. *You are the customer*, and you can find English teachers who will do what you ask them to. They do not have to be native-English speakers for you to learn.

Another good thing about this method is that you can start Globish where your last

学习全球语有很多方式。有些初学者们知道大约 350-500 个英语常用词汇，并且能够读和说这些词语。如果他们每天学习一个小时，包括练习说和写，那么大约要花费 6 个月的时间。六个月的时间，超过 120 天的学习时间，他们可以每天仅仅学习 10 个单词。那样应该不会太困难。

或许你无法就近获得全球语课程。但是如果你知道这本书中所给出的界限，那么你就可以指导一个当地的英语教师仅仅教你那些全球语词汇以及语句结构。你是客户，因此你可以找到愿意按你的要求去做的英语教师。对你的学习来说，他们不一定非要是英语母语人士。

这种方法的另一个好处是，你可以从上次停止英语学习的地

English stopped. If you start Globish knowing 1000 of the most-used English words, then it may take you only 3 *months* to master Globish. That is one of the best things about learning Globish. You know how much to do because you know where it will end.

There are Globish learning materials available. This book - in Globish - has the 1500 words and some other things you need to know. There are a number of materials on Globish already written in local languages or in Globish. There are also computer-based courses, and even a Globish course on a cell phone, the most widely available tool in the world. A lot of written and audio Globish can now be in your pocket or bag.

We should say a few words about pronunciation here. A good teacher can explain how to make clear English sounds.

方重新开始学习全球语。如果你在开始学习全球语之前知道 1000 个英语最常用的词汇，那么你可能只需要 3 个月就可以掌握全球语了。这就是学习全球语的最好的优点之一。因为你知道在哪里结束，所以你知道要做多少。

全球语的学习资料也可以利用。这本用全球语写的书包含 1500 个单词以及其他一些你需要知道的东西。在 Globish.com 网站上有许多用当地语言或全球语编写的材料。同时还有基于计算机的全球语教程，甚至在这种全世界应用最广泛的工具——手机上也有全球语课程。你现在可以将大量的全球语书面和音频资料放在你的口袋或包里。

这里我们应该就发音说几句。一个好的英语教师可以讲解如何清晰的发音。大多数教师都

Most teachers will also have audio for you to practice with those sounds. There is a lot of recorded material for learners to practice with. A lot of it is free on the radio, or the World Wide Web. And all of this audio is usually available with the most perfect English accent you can dream of. It can be the Queen's accent. It can be President Obama's accent. It can be whatever you want. Learners should hear different kinds of accents.

You have read here already that a perfect pronunciation is not needed, but only an understandable one, and that is plenty. You must believe this. After all, what is a *perfect accent?* London? Glasgow? Melbourne? Dallas? Toronto? Hollywood? Hong Kong? They *all* think they are perfect! Still, it is widely accepted that only native English speakers can really teach English, and that the teachers with another background should feel like second-class citizens. But this

会有让你练习的录音。初学者们有大量的录音材料可供练习。很多广播里或互联网上的材料都是免费的。而且这些录音材料里往往都是你做梦都想拥有的最完美的英语口音。它可以是女王式发音。它可以是奥巴马总统的口音。你想要什么样的都可以。初学者们应该听各种不同的口音。

当读到这里的时候，你应该已经明白你不需要完美的发音，但只要能让人听懂，那就足够了。你必须相信这一点。归根结底，哪里的口音是完美的？伦敦？格拉斯哥？墨尔本？达拉斯？多伦多？好莱坞？香港？他们都认为自己才是完美的！尽管如此，人们普遍认为只有英语母语人士才能真正的讲授英语，而那些来自不同背景的教师们就应该感觉像二等

world is changing...quickly.

Before this century, any native English speaker in any non-English-speaking city could sound like he or she knew much more about English, just by pronouncing English quickly and correctly. Non-native English teachers were sometimes worried that they were not well-qualified. They worried that people would discover their English was not perfect. There is good news now. Those days are gone. The old ideas might have been correct about English teaching in the year 1900, but not now. This is a new century. And Globish is the new language in town.

If you are such a teacher of English, things will change for you... all to the better.

If you are such a teacher: welcome to a world that really wants what you can do.

公民。但这个世界正在变化...迅速地。

这个世纪之前，只是因为能够很快的并正确的读出英语，任何一个英语母语人士在任何一个非英语国家的城市里都可以让人听起来好像他或她更加了解英语。母语非英语的英语教师们有时担心他们是否能胜任。他们担心人们会发觉他们的英语并不完美。现在有个好消息。那些日子已成过去。那些对于英语教学的老旧观念在 1900 年可能是对的，但不是现在。这是个新的世纪。而全球语是这个世界新的语言。

如果你是个这样的英语教师，那么事情将因你而改变...向着更好的方向。

如果你是个这样的教师。欢迎来到这个真正需要你所能做的世界。

Chapter 9
A Tool and... A Mindset

第九章

一个工具和... 一种心态

Globish can achieve what it does because it is useful English *without* a huge number of words and cultural idioms. If Globish speakers can use just this middle level of English, they will be respected everywhere in the world. But the most important difference between English and Globish is how we think when we use Globish.

全球语能够达到它的目标是因为它是有用的英语，不含有大量词汇及习语。假如说全球语的人可以使用这种中级英语，他们将会在世界各地得到尊重。但是英语和全球语之间最重要的不同点在于我们使用全球语时如何思考。

Who is responsible for effective communication? Is it the speaker and writer, or the listener and reader? The listener and reader cannot make communication good if the speaker or writer does not help. Who is guilty if the message does not get across? Who should do everything

谁应该为有效的沟通负责？是说写者，亦或是听读者？如果说写者不给予帮助，那么听读者就无法进行良好的沟通。如果信息没有传达给对方，那是谁的过错？谁应该尽一切可能确保对方理解自己说的话？

83

possible to make sure he or she is understood?

In English, the usual native speaker would answer: "Not me. I was born with English as a mother tongue, and I started listening to it – and learning it – in my mother's arms. If you do not understand me, it is your problem. My English is perfect. When yours gets better, you will not have the same difficulty. If you lack the drive to learn it, this is your problem, and not mine. English is the most important language. I am not responsible for that, but there is nothing I can do to make it different."

Globish is the complete opposite: the person who wants to talk must come at least half the distance to the person he talks to. He or she must decide what is necessary to make the communication happen. The native English speaker or the excellent speaker of English as a second language must

英语母语人士往往会用英语回答："不是我。我生来就会英语，这是我的母语，而且我在我母亲的怀抱里就开始听英语，学习英语。如果你听不懂我说的，那是你的问题。我的英语是完美的。等到你的英语变得更好的时候，你就不会像现在这么困难了。如果你缺乏学习英语的动力，那是你的问题，不是我的。英语是最重要的语言。我不用对此负责，但是我也不能做什么来改变它。"

全球语则完全相反：想要进行交谈的那个人必须与对方至少拉近一半的距离。他或她必须决定什么是进行沟通所必须的。英语母语人士或精通英语的非英语母语人士必须说："现在我必须用全球语水平的英语交谈，这样才可以使另一

84

say: "Today I must speak at the Globish level so this other person can understand me. If my listeners do not understand me, it is because I am not using the Globish tool very well. This is my responsibility, not theirs." Of course, not everyone accepts the idea of Globish yet. Perhaps they never heard about it. Perhaps they could never find the time to learn about it. Or perhaps they did not think they needed it.

Even if there are just two people, if this communication is important, Globish will help. This means you – the speaker – will take responsibility, using simple Globish words in a simple way, and using Globish "best practices" including body language and charts or pictures we can see. Most of all, when using Globish, the speaker should to wait for the listeners, to check they understand.

If there is a group of people, maybe only one does not

个人理解我的意思。如果我的听众听不懂我说的话，那是因为我没有很好的使用全球语这个工具。这是我的责任，不是他们的。"当然，目前为止并不是每个人都接受全球语的理念。或许他们从未曾听说过。或许他们从未曾有时间来学习全球语。或者可能他们认为自己并不需要。

如果沟通很重要，即使只有两个人，那么全球语就会起到帮助。这意味着你——说话者——要承担责任，以简单的方式使用简单的全球语词汇，以及使用全球语的"最好方法"，包括我们能看见的肢体语言和图表或图画。最重要的是，在使用全球语时，说话者应该等候听众，确认他们是否理解。

也许在一群人中，只有一个人不会说全球语。说话者可以想

speak Globish. The speaker can think: "This person is the only one in the group who can not understand or communicate in Globish. That is too bad. I will ask one of the others to help that one by explaining what was said in this discussion."

So sometimes we decide it is better to communicate with those who understand, and let them tell any others. This means it is good to stop now and then, so the other persons can learn what was said. The English speakers will understand anyway, and the below-Globish level will not at all, but you must work with the identified Globish group until you succeed. If you do not communicate with those, the failure will be yours.

On the other hand, there will be times when you are with native English speakers who do not know about the Globish guidelines, never heard of them, or just don't want to hear about it. But it is

到："这个人是这群人中唯一一个不能理解而且不能用全球语交流的人。这太糟糕了。我会让其他人中的一员来帮助他，把这次讨论的内容解释给他听。"

因此有时我们决定最好与那些能够听懂的人交流，之后让他们告诉其他人。这就意味着时不时的停下是有好处的，这样其他人就可以了解到说了什么。英语母语人士无论如何都会理解，而低于全球语水平的人将什么都听不懂，但你必须与懂得全球语的人们协作直至成功。如果你不与那些人沟通，那就是你的失败。

另一方面，有些时候你会和英语母语人士在一起，而他们对全球语的指导方针一无所知，从来没有听说过，或者只是不想听说。但是否将讨论引到正

up to you to bring the discussion to the correct level. This is in your best interest, but it is also your duty, because many of the members of this group may already be lost in this discussion.

You must now be their Globish leader. They will be more than thankful to you for bringing the matter into the open without fear. It is easy. Many English speakers forget about others or just do not think about them. You just have to raise a hand, wave it until you are noticed, and say: "Excuse me, I am sorry but some of us do not understand what you are saying. We need to understand you. Could you please repeat, in Globish please, this time?"

To be sure, you will have a reaction, and your native-speaker friend might understand the point for the rest of his or her life. You will have done a great service. But

确的水平就取决于你了。这都是为了你好，但同时也是你的义务，因为这群人中的很多成员可能已经在这场讨论中迷失了。

现在你必须成为他们的全球语带头人。对于你无所畏惧的将此事公开，他们对你的感激将无法言表。这很简单。许多英语母语人士忘记了其他人或者根本就不考虑他们。你只需要举起一只手，不停地挥动直到被别人注意到，然后说："对不起，打扰一下，但是我们中有些人听不懂您在说什么。我们需要理解您的话。请问您这次是否可以用全球语重复一遍？"

无疑，你将会引起反响，而且你的英语母语人士朋友可能会在他或她的余生中领会这一点。你将会做出巨大的贡献。

the first reaction is most likely going to be a surprise: "Globish, what's that?" It will give you a fine opportunity to explain the story you now understand, and give its reasons. At best you will have an interested native speaker, who wants to know more, will understand your explanation, and will become a much better global communicator, and a Globish friend. That person will see that Globish is often better than English because it is much more sympathetic.

As we said, pronunciations are "acceptable" as soon as they are understood. A foreign accent is never a mistake; it is part of a person's special quality. It makes you different, and can even make you sound sexy. People who have reasonable Globish pronunciation can now stop trying to make it "better" – or to get closer to some native English speaker's – if they are understood.

但第一反应最有可能会是惊讶："全球语，那是什么？"这就会给你一个很好的机会去解释你现在理解的故事，并给出理由。最好的情况是这位英语母语人士会对此感兴趣，想要了解更多，会理解你的解释，并会成为一个更好的全球语传播者以及全球语的朋友。这个人会发现全球语往往要比英语更好，因为它更有人情味。

正如我们此前说的，只要别人能听懂你的发音，那就是"可以接受的"。拥有外国口音永远都不是个错误；它是一个人的一部分特质。它让你与众不同，甚至可以让你听起来很性感。只要能够被理解，那么拥有适当全球语发音的人们现在可以停止尝试让它变得"更好"—或者更贴近某些英语母语人士的发音。

We said Globish is still correct English. This means you are expected to write and speak in correct English. The grammar should be reasonable –about subjects and actions, time and place. Globish does not worry about very small differences in American and British speech or spelling or grammar. (And neither should anyone else.)

Globish is much more forgiving because it is asking for understanding, not perfect English. But there is an extra benefit in Globish to all native and non-native speakers: simplicity. It is what older politicians tell younger politicians about their first speeches. It is what older advertising people tell the bright younger ones about making a successful advertisement. It is what news editors tell their young writers about making a good news story. And it is what every English speaking professor should tell every non-native English student

我们说过全球语仍然是正确的英语。这意味你应该说写正确的英语。语法应该是适当的——关于主语和动作，时间，以及地点。全球语不会对美国英语和英国英语之间词汇，拼写，或语法上非常细小的差别有所顾虑。（而且任何人都不该有所顾虑。）

全球语更加宽松是因为它寻求理解，而不是完美的英语。但是全球语对于所有的英语母语人士和非英语母语人士都有个额外的好处：简明。这正是老练的政客告诫年轻的政治家在第一次演讲中要注意的。这正是资深的广告人告诉聪明的年轻人一个成功的广告中要具备的。这正是新闻编辑吩咐年轻的作家一篇好的新闻报道中要含有的。这也正是所有英语教授应该告诉每个非英语母语学生在说写时要注重的。

about writing and speaking.

On one side of the ocean, Winston Churchill said: "Never use a pound (£) word when a penny (1d) one will do"....

And a similar saying known to Americans:

K. I. S. S. =   Keep It Simple, Stupid.

在大洋彼岸，温斯顿·丘吉尔说过："不要大词小用"....

而美国人所熟知的一个相似的表达就是：

越简单约好

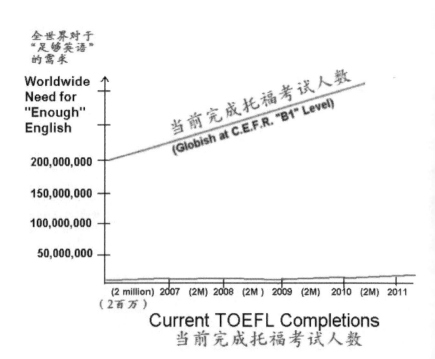

Current TOEFL Completions
当前完成托福考试人数

Chapter 10
Globish in Many Places

Globish has no desire to be a cultural language like French, or Chinese...or English. People who will use Globish already have their own respected culture and their own language. They will use Globish only as a tool, but it will be the chosen tool of a huge majority of people around the world. When they see ahead to this future many non-native English speakers will decide this is still English. And it is really a form of English, a clear form of that language. They may fear that English is winning over everything they love. They may see this as a threat to their own mother tongue and their culture. So they might decide that they have to fight for the survival of

第十章
全球语遍布各地

全球语不愿成为像法语，汉语，或英语那样的文化语言。将要使用全球语的人们已经拥有了他们所尊敬的文化以及他们自己的语言。他们只会将全球语作为一个工具来使用，但全世界绝大多数人都会选择全球语这个工具。当他们展望未来的时候，许多非英语母语人士会决定这仍然是英语。而且它确实是英语的一种形式，一种清晰地形式。他们可能恐惧英语正在征服他们热爱的一切。他们可能认为这会威胁到他们的母语及他们的文化。所以他们可能下决心不得不为了他们的故乡和热爱的语言——

their French, Japanese, Russian or Tagalog – their home and beloved language. Each of them is a respected cultural language for many people.

This threat could be true IF we were advising you to learn English. That would be helping English compete with other cultural languages. A few cultures have already taken extreme steps because they fear that the English culture will replace their own. They feel it brings poor values and takes away the strength of their own culture.

However, advising you to learn Globish does the opposite. Globish cannot have any cultural goals, so it does not threaten anyone's language or anyone's culture. It replaces the English competition. Using only Globish could keep all these wonderful cultures *safer* from the English cultural invasion.

Globish can also protect the English language from being

法语，日语，俄语，或菲律宾语的生存而奋斗。它们中的每一个都是受到许多人尊敬的文化语言。

如果我们建议您学习英语，那么这种威胁可能成真。这将会帮助英语同其他文化语言相竞争。一些文化已经采取了极端措施因为他们害怕英语文化会取代他们自己的文化。他们觉得英语会带来低劣的价值观并带走他们自身文化的优势。

然而，建议您学习全球语则完全相反。全球语不可能有任何文化目的，所以它不会威胁任何人的语言或文化。它取代了英语竞赛。仅使用全球语可以阻止所有这些灿烂的文化受到英语的文化侵略，从而更安全。

全球语也可以保护英语语言不

"broken" by other cultures. English is a very special case today. In fact, the non-native English speakers who use English are far more numerous than native English speakers. So the non-native speakers will decide and lead in the future of the English language. They will create and present new words, and will throw away the old words. This will happen unless the Globish idea becomes an accepted tool. If this happens, it will give the English language a chance to survive as a cultural language.

Globish offers the English-speaking countries a chance to say: We have a wonderful language, linked to a wonderful culture, and we would like to save all of that. However, we accept that international communication today is mostly using our language. But we can divide the language in two parts. One form will be for English culture that is ours, and one form will be for global

被其他文化所"破坏"。英语的现状非常特殊。事实上，使用英语的非英语母语人士在数量上要比英语母语人士多得多。因此非英语母语人士将会决定并引导未来英语的发展。他们将会创造并提出新的词汇，而且会将旧的词语丢弃。这种情况将会发生，除非全球语成为公认的工具。如果全球语成功了，那么英语将会得到一个机会，继续以文化语言生存下去。

全球语为英语国家提供了一个发言的机会：我们拥有一个奇妙的语言，它连接着一个灿烂的文化，而且我们想要拯救所有这些。无论如何，我们相信今天的大部分国际交流使用的是我们的语言。但是我们可以将这种语言分为两个部分。一种形式将是我们的英语文化，而另一种形式将被用于国际间

communication, trade, and traveling (and this is Globish, with exact rules.) We will attempt to use this second form - Globish - whenever we are in those other worlds which are not part of the English culture (s). And we are the lucky ones…Learning Globish for us will be much easier than learning a new language for each place.

交流，贸易，和旅游（而这就是带有严格规范的全球语。）当我们身处于非英语国家时，我们将尝试使用第二种形式——全球语。而且我们就是幸运儿…对我们来说学习全球语比每去一个国家就学习一种新的语言要简单得多。

(Relative Daily English Needs)
（相对日常英语需求）

If you are delivering a speech in front of a large international audience, you have to deal with many different levels of English. You might think they are like one person, but each individual has different abilities.

On top of that, someone will be recording you, and your

如果你在一大批国际听众面前做演讲，那么你不得不面对许多英语水平不同的人。你或许会将他们视为同一个人，但是每个人都有不同的能力。

除此之外，有人会给你录音，而且人们可以通过很多途径看到你的表现，包括电视，因

94

performance will be available in many ways, including on the TV and on the Internet and on DVDs. You need to be understood quickly by the largest possible number. You might think that excellent speakers of two languages are the answer. Interpreters give second-by-second changes to the audience in their languages. But even that method is much better with Globish than with English. The Globish limitations and especially its simpler sentences, shorter and lighter, all ensure better correctness when the speech is changed to another language.

Ask any interpreter: Their worst experience is the long, involved sentences where they get lost. This person needs to listen to all of the words to get the meaning, and if the talk is too long, he or she has lost the beginning when the end finally comes. But those kinds of statements-within-statements

特网，以及 DVD 光碟。你需要很快的让尽可能多的人听懂你的话。你或许会认为精通两种语言的人可以解决问题。然而口译者翻译给听众的语言每时每刻都在改变原意。但即使同样是这种方法，用全球语也要比用英语更好。全球语的局限性，特别是它更加容易的句子，简短而且一目了然，在翻译成其他语言时保证了更高的准确性。

询问任何一个口译者：他们最糟糕的经历就是那些让他们不知所措的冗长复杂的句子。为了领会意思，口译者需要仔细听所有的词语，然而如果一句话太长，当结尾来临的时候，他或她已经忘了开头的意思。但这种句子包含句子的表

are mistakes in Globish.

The other horrible experience of the interpreters is seeing words used differently in a field or subject that they don't know. In English there is the word "program", and it means very different things on the TV and on the computer. The interpreter who does not know the field completely will make too many mistakes. On the other hand, if you are talking in Globish, many people in the audience will choose to listen directly to you. The simplest solution is to say things in Globish. You can then use special "technical words" – along with pictures to support them – in a way that people in the industry will quickly understand.

It is very difficult to use Globish guidelines while you are creating your words right there in front of people. But once you are familiar with the idea, practice makes it easier within a short time. The safest way, however, is

达方式在全球语中是错误的。

口译者的另一个可怕经历就是在他们不了解的领域或专业中遇到一些有不同用法的词语。英语中有个词"程序",但它在电视和电脑领域的意思却非常不同。对此领域不是完全了解的口译者会犯太多错误。另一方面,如果你使用全球语进行演讲,听众中的很多人会选择直接听你的讲话。最简单的方案就是通过全球语来表达。然后你可以使用特殊的"专业术语"——连同支撑它们的图片——这种方法可以让业内人士迅速理解。

当你在众人面前构思的时候,要遵守全球语的指导方针是非常困难的。但是只要你熟悉了这个概念,通过实践在很短的时间内就可以掌握。然而,最安全的方法就是按照一

to give a speech from a written text, and go over that text with Globish software. It will improve the "hit rate" of the speech (a technical term for the percent of people who listen and do understand). Usually it is at least three times better, and ten times with some listeners who are *not* native English speakers.

A good example is the excellent video tape to the Iranian people by President Obama in 2009. It was in Globish-like language and it could be understood by much of the world without translation. They also listened to Obama's same words in Jerusalem and Ramallah, in Istanbul and in Seoul. In too many other cases, however, major international speeches are made at a level of English that is too difficult for non-native speakers. Of course those international speakers think they did their job. They are wrong. Their job was to be understood by all their

篇写好的版本进行演讲，用全球语法则将文章重说一遍。这会提高演讲的"命中率"（一个形容听懂人数所占百分比的专业术语）。通常效果至少提高三倍，而对于一些非英语母语听众来说效果能提高十倍。

一个典型的例子就是 2009 年奥巴马总统致伊朗人民讲话的精彩录像。这段演讲用的是类似全球语的语言，而且世界上的大部分人不用翻译都可以听懂。在耶路撒冷和拉马拉的人们，在伊斯坦布尔和首尔的人们都听了奥巴马相同的讲话。然而，在其他许多情况下，主要的国际演讲中使用的英语水平对于非英语母语人士来说太高了。当然这些国际演说家们认为他们已经尽了他们的职责。那他们就错了。他们的职责是让他们所有的听众都能听

97

listeners.

If you are a native English speaker, you could argue that things are very different when you write. You know who you are writing to, and you know that his or her English is very good. Perhaps you write to that person with difficult words to show your ability with the language. But this could be another huge mistake. Very often good ideas are passed on as is to others. You should know that whatever you write today is not written just for the person you send it to. It is always written for the whole wide world. And for this reason, it should be in Globish. If it is forwarded through the Internet it can go around the world 4000 times before you finish your next call. The problem is, if they don't understand it, they will still try to pick up a few words and tell that to their friends. And then what you didn't say well they will say even more poorly in 5000 other

懂。

如果你是英语母语人士，那么你可能会争辩说当你写东西的时候情况会非常不同。因为你知道你要写给谁，而且也知道他或她的英语非常好。或许你写给那个人的信中含有很难的词语是为了显示你的语言能力。但是这有可能是另一个巨大的错误。好的想法往往人们都会互相传递。你应该知道今天无论你写了什么并不只是写给那个人的。同样是为整个世界而写的。正因如此，这封信应该用全球语来写。如果是通过英特网发送的话，在你打完下一通电话之前，这封信可以绕地球转 4000 圈了。问题是，如果他们不明白，他们仍然会试图挑出一些词语，然后告诉他们的朋友。于是，那些你说得不好的东西甚至会被他们用另外 5000 种语言更糟糕

languages. The good news is that now you can talk to the whole world at the speed of light. But the really bad news is that no one will ever tell you they don't understand. They would be ashamed to show their limitations, so they will all say back to you: "Oh yes, it was very interesting."

You could be working for a global company, with shares owned by people from 123 different countries. They speak almost as many languages. Look closely at your yearly report, and at all the papers sent to shareholders. It is probably written in wonderful English which non-native English speakers from the 117 non-English speaking countries can almost understand. Or is it written in Globish, using exactly the same numbers and saying exactly the same things, but understandable by many more of those shareholders?

If you work in a government

的重复下去。好消息是你现在能够以光速与全世界交流。但真正的坏消息是没有人会告诉你他们不明白。他们会因为显出自己的不足而感到羞耻，所以他们都会回答你："哦，是的，非常有趣。"

你可能在一家跨国企业工作，而这家企业的股东来自 123 个不同的国家。他们几乎都说不同的语言。仔细看看你写的年报以及发给股东的所有文件。或许这些文件是用精彩的英语写成的，而且来自 117 个非英语国家的非英语母语人士可以差不多看懂。 或者这些文件是用全球语写成的，使用完全一样的数字而且陈述完全一样的事情，但却能够被更多的股东看懂？

如果你在一个英语国家的政府

agency in an English speaking country, look at the papers and forms for the citizens. Many people –who are new to the country and to your language – will have to fill in those forms. They should reach the Globish level soon, and that may be fairly easy. But then, they should get papers written only in Globish, which are understandable *both* by these new ones *and* by all the English-speaking citizens. It would cost much less than printing every paper and form in many different languages. And new people could perform better and more quickly in the economy if they could read the language. Globish can fill this need, but that nation must make this standard, and demonstrate it in all its important papers.

There will always be a few of the new people who cannot yet operate in Globish, even to read simple writing. They may still need to see something in their languages.

机关工作，那么看看那些为公民们准备的文件和表格。许多对这个国家及其语言还不熟悉的人们将不得不填写这些表格。这些表格应该很快达到全球语的水平，而那样或许相当容易。 此外，人们应该得到仅用全球语写的文件，这些文件可以让新移民以及所有的英语母语公民都看得懂。这比用许多不同的语言印刷每份文件和表格要便宜很多。而且如果他们可以读懂那种语言，那么新来的移民就能够在经济建设中更快更好的做出贡献。全球语可以满足这种需求，但是那个国家必须制定标准，并且在其所有的重要文件中使用。

始终会有一些新人仍然无法理解全球语，甚至无法阅读简单的文件。他们也许还需要读用他们的语言书写的文件。从标

From normal English the usual solution would be many translators, one for each language. Their work might be excellent, but it would take a lot of time and a lot of money.

You could also decide to have computer translations to these languages from English. But you must make sure that it works; here is how to do that. Have the computer translate part of your English version into – say – Poldevian. When you have a result, do not show it immediately to the Poldevians. Instead, order the computer to change the Poldevian document back to English. If you think you can understand it – and accept it – then the process is good. In most cases you will be surprised in a bad way. You will decide that computers cannot change languages very well yet. However, Globish has a much better chance of giving good results in computer translation. It has simpler sentence

准英语的方面来看，常见的解决方法是使用很多译员，每种语言一个。他们的效果可能非常显著，但这也会花费大量时间和金钱。

你也可以决定用电脑将英语翻译成这些语言。但你必须确保这招管用；这么做的方法是：用电脑将英文版本的一部分翻译成，例如 Poldevian 语（此种语言系作者虚构）。当你得到结果之后，不要立即拿给这个国家的人看。相反，命令电脑将文件翻译回英文。如果你觉得你能够理解并接受，那么这就是个好的方法。但在大多数情况下，结果会让你大吃一惊。那时你会拿定主意，电脑还不能很好的转换语言。然而，用电脑翻译全球语，得到好的结果的可能性更大。全球语的句子结构更简单，而且使用最常见的英语词汇。很多时

structures, and uses the most common English words. Many times, the computer translation from Globish to Poldevian will give better results, but not perfect results. This is true of most of Globish, where the goal is to create understanding without 100% perfection.

We must remember, however, that Globish is not a holy language. It is an idea, a guidance. The better you keep to it, the more people will understand you. Perhaps it is like a diet. The closer you stay to it, the more weight you lose. But no diet is going to fail if – just a few times – you have a glass of wine, or a beer. Off-limits words in Globish are not wrong; it is just not wise to bring in difficult words too often. You can use a rare word because no other one will do, and many readers will run to their word books. Or you can use two Globish words that are widely understood by your readers or listeners... and mean the same thing. It

候用电脑将全球语翻译成 Poldevian 能够得到更好的结果,但并不是完美的。这对于大部分全球语而言是正确的,因为我们的目标就是创造没有100%完美的理解力。

然而,我们必须记住的是全球语不是一种神圣的语言。它是一种思想,一种引导。你越是坚持使用它,就会有越多的人理解你。也许这就像节食。你坚持的时间越长,你减掉的体重就越多。但是即使你偶尔喝一杯葡萄酒或啤酒,节食也不会因此而失败。超出全球语范围的词汇并不是错误的;只不过太频繁的引入难以理解的词语是不明智的。你可以使用一个别人不会用的罕见的词,结果许多读者都会去求助于他们的单词书。或者你可以使用你的读者或听众广泛接受的两个

is up to you. But the more you stay with the guidance, the better chance you have of everyone understanding you.

It is clear also that people who decide to use Globish will possibly master many more words than the list given here. This is clearly true for advanced English students, of course, but also for the other speakers. In many cases the non-native speakers will hear speech or see written material that uses more difficult words. In most cases, non-native speakers will learn these new words, and have them available in case they need to use them again later. This is a good result. We are not suggesting that people close their eyes and their ears to all new words. And there will often be native English speakers who reject the Globish idea completely. With this kind of people, more words will always help the non-native

全球语词汇，而且表达的意思一样。这由你来决定。然而，你越是遵守全球语的指导方针，就会有越多的机会让每个人都理解你。

显而易见的是决定使用全球语的人们很有可能掌握比这本书中列出的单词表还要多得多的词汇。当然，不仅对于高水平的英语学生而言尤其如此，而且对于说其他语言的人也是一样。在许多情况下，非英语母语人士会在演讲中听到或在书面材料中读到更加难以理解的词语。大多数情况下，非英语母语人士会学习这些新词，并记住它们以防今后还会再次用到。这就是个不错的结果。我们并不是建议人们对所有的新词视而不见听而不闻。而且经常会有英语母语人士完全抵制全球语思想。与这类人交流时，更大的词汇量总会对非英

speakers to understand.

But these borders of this Globish "middle ground" are not made to keep people in or out. If all speakers know they can come back and be welcomed into Globish, then communication has a chance.

语母语人士的理解有所帮助。

但是全球语"中间地带"的这些边界并不是用来束缚人们的。如果所有的人都知道他们可以重新使用全球语而且是受欢迎的，那么沟通就有机会了。

Technical Words

Interpreter - a person who tells the meaning in one language to those who speak another language.

Translation - Changing of one language to another. Sometime human translators are called interpreters as well.

Part 2
Elements of
Globish

第二部分

全球语要素

(1500 words, 6-10 verb-time formations, phrasal verbs, 8 parts of speech, plus Active, Passive, Conditional forms. Best: 15-word sentences, Maximum 26 word sentences)

（1500 个单词，6-10 种动词时态构成，动词短语，8 种词性，加上主动、被动语态，条件句。句子长度最好少于 15 个词的，最多不要超过 26 个词）

Chapter 11
How Much Is "Enough"?

Globish is "enough" English. That is why a person can learn it more quickly than full English. There are many structures, rules, and ways of using English which make it difficult. Globish has limits so that it is easier to learn and start speaking. A person can know exactly *what* to learn. This is also very helpful in communication between people of varying English abilities. They can all know what to say and write.

But the question will always be asked: "What does "enough" mean? What is "enough?" "Not enough" means that you cannot communicate comfortably with anyone, in English or

第十一章
多少算"足够"？

全球语是"足够的"英语。这就是为什么一个人学习全球语可以比学习全部英语要更快。英语中许多的结构、规则、和使用方法使其变的很难。全球语因其有局限性所以更容易学习并开口说话。一个人可以确切地知道要学习什么。这对于英语水平不同的人互相之间进行交流也非常有帮助。他们都能够知道要说什么以及要写什么。

但是总会有人问这个问题："'足够'是什么意思？什么是'足够'？""不够"的意思是无论用英语还是全球语，你都不能舒适地与任何人交流。可能是因为

Globish. You may not know enough words or - more likely - you do not say words with the right stresses, or you may not know simple sentence forms and verb forms. So how much is "too much?" "Too much" makes many students learning English feel they will "never be good enough" in English.

The Council of Europe offers a *Common European Framework of Reference for Languages* (C.E.F.R.) that offers a situational test for users of all second languages. By their standard, the best user of Globish would be an Independent User (Their category called "B1") THIS IS GIVEN EXACTLY IN C.E.F.R.'s ENGLISH:

> *Can understand the main points of clear standard input on familiar matters regularly encountered in work, school, leisure, etc. Can deal with most situations likely to arise whilst travelling in an area where the language is*

你没有掌握足够的词汇或者更有可能的是，你说话时的重音不对，或者有可能你不知道简单的句式或动词的形式。那么多少又是"太多"呢？"太多"就是让许多英语学习者们感觉他们的英语"永远都不够好"。

欧洲议会提出的*欧洲共同语言参考标准*（C.E.F.R.）包含为所有第二语言使用者设计的情境测试。根据他们的标准，全球语说的最好的人是独立使用者（他们的标准称其为"B1"）以下完全是用 C.E.F.R.的英语表达的：

> 对于通常在工作、学习、休闲等场合遇到的熟悉事物，能够理解以清晰标准语言所表达的要点。能在该语言使用地区旅游时应对大多数可能发生的状

108

spoken.

Can produce simple connected text on topics, which are familiar, or of personal interest. Can describe experiences and events, dreams, hopes & ambitions and briefly give reasons and explanations for opinions and plans.

That is the test for "enough" for their B1 - Independent User. It would be enough for the Globish user too, if we added this:

"Uses all words needed to join in a given profession or activity; uses International words appropriate in all travel or international business situations."

But many Globish users can operate at the higher Level B2 of that same C.E.F.R. Independent User standard:

"Can understand the main ideas of complex text on both concrete and abstract topics, including technical discussions in his/her field of

况。

针对熟悉的或私人感兴趣的话题，可以表达简单而连贯的内容。能够叙述经验，事件，梦想，希望以及志向，并能简短地对看法和计划陈述理由及做出说明。

这就是为他们的 B1——独立使用者准备的"足够"测验。 如果我们加上这些，那么对于全球语使用者来说也足够了：

能够使用加入特定职业或活动所需的所有词汇 ；能够在所有旅行及国际商务环境中恰当地使用国际化词语。

但是许多全球语使用者的能力已经达到了等同于 C.E.F.R.独立使用者的 B2 水平：

不论具体或抽象的话题，对于其复杂的内容都能够了解主旨，包括个人专业领域

specialisation. Can interact with a degree of fluency and spontaneity that makes regular interaction with native speakers quite possible without strain for either party. Can produce clear, detailed text on a wide range of subjects and explain a viewpoint on a topical issue giving the advantages and disadvantages of various options."

So there are people who have been thinking about this Globish "level" of language use. There are many, many more who have been using something quite close to Globish. Even with few written standards, some have called it Globish because they feel their level of usage is "Globish." They are using the word "Globish" to establish a level of comfort - a middle ground to communicate with others. Now we hope they can be even more certain because of the observations in this book.

At the risk of saying some important things once again, we will now unite some

的技术性讨论。能够一定程度流利地并且自然地进行互动，与母语人士经常交流，双方都不会感到紧张。能够针对各种不同的主题表达清晰详细的内容，可针对热点问题解释其观点并说明不同论点的优劣。

因此有人一直在思考全球语的这种语言运用"水平"。还有更多人一直在使用与全球语相近的语言。有的甚至还有书面标准，有人称其为全球语因为他们认为他们的水平达到了"全球语"的标准。他们使用"全球语"名字是想要建立一种舒适感——一个可以与他人进行交流的中间地带。现在我们希望他们能够因为这本书中的言论而更加确信。

再次冒险说一些重要的事情，我们现在将要整合这本书第一

110

observations from the first part of the book. This will lay the groundwork for describing major language elements that are important to Globish.

First we will review the ways Globish is like English and then how Globish differs from English. Then, we will examine what makes this Closed System of Natural Language an effective tool for world communication.

English speakers may well say: If Globish is like English, why not just learn English? But there are certain things English speakers do not try to understand. That is one of the main reasons people in many places will be speaking Globish.

部分中的一些言论。这将为描述那些对于全球语很重要的主要语言要素打下基础。

首先我们将回顾一下全球语同英语的相似之处，之后是它们之间的不同之处。然后，我们将审视是什么让这个自然语言的封闭系统成为全世界交流的有效工具。

英语母语人士完全可以这么说：如果全球语像英语，那为什么不直接学习英语？但是有些事情是英语母语人士不愿尝试去理解的。这就是为什么很多地方的人们都将说全球语的主要原因之一。

Chapter 12
Is Globish the Same as English?

Globish is correct English

Native English speakers can easily read and understand this book. But because of this, English speakers do not always notice that Globish is not just **any** English. They can miss the value of limiting their English to Globish. It should instead be a comfort to them, that what they are reading can also be easily understood by Globish speakers as well.

In reading this book, all English-speakers are observing a "common ground" *in action*. Most probably as many as one and a half billion other people can read and understand this

第十二章
全球语和英语是相同的吗？

全球语是正确的英语

英语母语人士能够轻松的阅读并理解这本书。但正因如此，说英语的人往往没有注意到全球语并不是**随便的**英语。他们可能因而忽视将他们的英语控制在全球语水平的重要性。这对于他们来说反而应该是一种安慰，因为说全球语的人同样能够轻松地理解他们正在阅读的东西。

在阅读这本书的时候，所有说英语的人都注意到一个"中间地带"在起作用。很可能有多达十五亿人能够阅读并理解这同一本书。

113

same book.

Of course, at first it might seem that all English speakers can use Globish almost without thinking. However, English speakers who want to speak and write Globish must do four things: (1) use short sentences; (2) use words in a simple way; as any advertiser or politician knows; (3) use only the most common English words, and (4) help communication with body language and visual additions. Also, they must find ways to repeat what they decide is very important.

Globish spelling is English spelling

Most English speakers have trouble with their own spelling, because the English words come from many cultures. There are probably more exceptions to the rules than there are rules. Often, people learn to spell English words by memory: they *memorize* what the word *looks like*.

当然，最初看起来所有英语母语人士都能几乎不加思索的使用全球语。但想要说写全球语，英语母语人士必须做到以下四点：（1）使用短句；（2）以简单的方法使用词语，就像广告商和政治家那样；（3）使用最常见的英语词汇，（4）运用肢体语言及可视附件帮助交流。另外，他们必须寻找途径重复重要的事情。

全球语拼写是英语拼写

大多数英语母语人士自己的拼写都有问题，因为英语词汇来自许多不同文化。例外可能比规则还要多。通常，人们是通过记忆来学习拼写英语单词：他们记住某个词的样子。

Globish sounds like English

Globish speakers must learn to stress parts of words correctly. If the stress is correct, the word is most easily understood. It does not matter so much about the accent. And some sounds that are hard to make do not matter so much. A second problem in pronunciation is easier: the *schwa* sound can often be a substitute in most parts of words that are *not* stressed. (More in Chapter 16).

Globish uses the same letters, markings and numbers as English

It also has the same days, months and other time and place forms.

全球语听起来像英语

说全球语的人必须学习如何读准重音。如果一个词的重音发准了，那么就最容易被人理解。口音并没有那么重要。而且有些很难发出的单音也无关紧要。发音的第二个问题比较容易：中元音常常可以替代大多数非重读音节。（将在第 16 章中详细讨论）。

全球语使用的字母，标点，和数字与英语相同

而且星期，月份，以及其他表达时间和地点的格式也都是相同的。

Globish uses the basic grammar of English, with fewer Tenses, Voices, and Moods.

全球语使用英语的基本语法；而时态，语态，和语气种类都较少。

Technical Words

Capitalize - put a large letter at the first of the word.

Visual - can be seen with the eyes

Tenses - the time a verb shows, Present, Pa st, or Future order.

Voice - a type of grammar. We use Active voice most in Globish.

Moods - ways of speaking. Imperative Mood: *"Don't look at me!"*

Directions – Globish/English
发展方向 – 全球语 / 英语

（能够在全世界90%的工作、旅行环境中进行交流）(Communicate in 90% of work, travel situations WWide)

(Little value without 3-5 more years of classes) （没有超过3-5年的课程学习就没有多大价值）

12 mo
12个月

English

Globish

6个月

1. 1500 Words plus 3500 children
1500个基本词汇加3500个衍生词汇

2. Simple Verb forms
简单的动词形式

3. No Idioms
不用习语

1. Cultural Words from English Speaking Countries.
来自英语国家的文化词语

2. Numerous added Verb forms
大量额外的动词形式

3. Numerous Idioms
大量习语

Early Globish classes deal with basic words and pronunciation, simple present, past, future verbs, questions, parts of speech.
初期全球语课程涉及基本词汇和发音，一般现在时，一般过去时，一般将来时的动词，疑问句，词性。

Early Globish and English quite similar
全球语和英语早期非常相似。

Early English classes deal with basic words and pronunciation, simple present, past, future verbs, questions, parts of speech.
初期英语课程涉及基本词汇和发音，一般现在时，一般过去时，一般将来时的动词，疑问句，词性。

G E

Chapter 13
How Globish is Different from English

Globish has a different name

The name lets people know exactly how much English they are using. It also lets native English speakers know that they do not "own" this language. Globish means we use the same simple rules for everyone. And it usually means that the speaker or writer is trying to help with understanding. Globish speakers enjoy the fact that all cultures are talking *together*.

第十三章
全球语和英语有什么不同

全球语有个不同的名字

这个名字让人们确切地了解他们正使用多少英语。这也让英语母语人士知道他们并不"拥有"这个语言。全球语意味着我们让每个人都使用同样简单的规则。而且这通常指的是说话者或作者正试图帮助理解。说全球语的人享受所有文化在一起交流这个事实。

Globish has 1500 words, expandable in four ways:

- different use of same word,
- combinations of words,
- short additions to words,
- and Phrasal Verbs.

Also allowed are (a) Names and Titles - (capitalized), (b) international words like *police* and *pizza*, (c) technical words like *noun* and *grammar* in this book. Only common agreement between speakers can decide between them, of course, what other words to allow beyond these 1500 Globish words. If one person cannot understand an additional word, then its use is not recommended. (See Chapters 16 and 17).

全球语拥有 1500 个词汇，可通过以下四种方式扩展：

- 同一个词的不同使用方法，
- 词语的组合，
- 对词语进行简短地增添
- 以及动词短语

其他被认可的还有：（a）名字和称号-（大写的）；（b）国际词汇，如*警察*和*比萨饼*；（c）专业术语，例如本书中的*名词*和*语法*。当然，只有说话者之间达成一致才可以确定超出这 1500 个全球语词汇范围的词语。如果其中有一个人不能理解一个额外的词，那么不建议再使用那个词。（见第 16 和 17 章）

Globish uses mostly Active Voice

Globish speakers should understand Passive and Conditional forms. But it is usually best for Globish users to create messages in Active Voice if possible. Who or what is doing the action must be clear in Globish. English may say:

> *The streets were cleaned in the morning.*

But Globish would say:

> *The workmen cleaned the streets in the morning.*

Globish suggests short sentences (15 words or fewer)

This limits phrases and clauses, but allows them if necessary. Instead of:

> *When we went to Paris we took a nice*

全球语主要使用主动语态

说全球语的人应该懂得被动语态和条件句形式。但如果可能的话，通常全球语使用者最好使用主动语态来传达信息。在全球语中必须清楚谁或什么发出动作。英语可能会说：

> *早晨街道被打扫干净了。*

但用全球语会说：

> *早晨工人们把街道打扫干净了。*

全球语建议使用简短的句子（15个词或更少）

这限制了短语和从句，但必要时还是允许使用它们的。与其说：

> *当我们去巴黎的时*

119

little hotel not far from the main shopping area so that we would not have too far to carry our purchases.

候我们住在一家很好的距离主要商业区不远的小旅馆为的是购物之后我们不需要拎着东西走很远的路。

Globish speakers will say:

全球语使用者会说：

We went to Paris, and we found a nice little hotel. It was near the main shopping area. That way, we would not have too far to carry our purchases.

我们去了巴黎，然后我们发现了一家很好的小旅馆。它距离主要商业区很近。那样的话，购物之后我们就不需要拎着东西走很远的路了。

Globish pronunciation has fewer necessary sounds than traditional English

全球语发音中必需的单音比传统英语更少

Globish sounds should be learned with each word. Most important: Globish must use syllable stress VEry corRECTly. Because there are similar sounds in most

全球语的发音需要通过每个词语来学习。最重要的是：说全球语时重读音节必须非常准确。因为大多数语言的发音都

languages, each speaker may have to learn only a few new sounds. (See Chapter 21).

有相似之处，每个人可能只需要学习几种新的单音。（见第21章）

Globish speakers use their body, their hands and their face when they talk

说全球语的人在交谈时使用他们的身体，他们的手臂，和他们的面部表情

They use headlines, **dark print**, underline, and pictures with written Globish. In meetings, Globish speakers use objects, pictures, sounds, and give things to the listeners. Good Globish speakers speak clearly, and are happy to repeat what they have said. Globish speakers check that the listeners understand before they say the next thing. They repeat all questions AND answers in meetings. (More in Chapter 18)

在用全球语写作时，他们使用大标题，**黑体字**，下划线，以及图片。在开会时，说全球语的人使用实物，图片，声音，并且让听众实践。全球语说得好的人讲话很清晰，而且非常乐意重复他们说过的话。说全球语的人在说下一件事情之前会核实听众们是否已经理解。他们在开会时会重复所有的问题和答案。（我们将在第18章中详细讨论）

Globish speakers are very careful about humor, idioms and examples

Globish speakers can have fun, and be friendly. But they avoid anything that might not be understood. Most people are careful not to use the same humor with their parents and their friends. Sometimes humor is good for one person but offensive to another. This is even more difficult to know about between cultures, so it is best to avoid trying to be "funny". In the same way, examples from one culture might not be good in another culture and some analogies might not carry exactly the same meaning. And idioms, things that depend on understanding a certain culture, should be avoided. (More in Chapter 19)

说全球语的人对待幽默，习语和例子非常谨慎

说全球语的人可以很有趣，可以很友好。但他们避免任何有可能理解不了的东西。大多数人很小心且不会在父母和朋友面前用相同的幽默。有时同一个幽默对某个人来说很好但却会冒犯另一个人。对于不同文化来说这一点更难理解，所以最好避免尝试"富于幽默"。同样地，某个文化中的例子在另一个文化中可能就不那么贴切了，而且有些比喻可能就不那么恰当了。同时，应该避免使用习语这样需要理解某种文化的东西。（我们将在第 19 章中详细讨论）

Globish is a "Closed System of Natural Language."

This is what makes Globish useful, dependable, and easier to learn and use. The next chapters will be about "natural language" and Globish's closed system.

全球语是一个"自然语言的封闭系统"

这一点使得全球语有用，可靠，而且易学易用。下一章将会讨论"自然语言"和全球语的封闭系统。

Technical words

Noun - a part of speech naming a person, place, or thing.

Passive Voice - a sentence with n o subject. "The house is sold."

Active Voice - usual sentence - subject first. "Mary came home."

Figurative - expressing one thing in terms of another: "on thin ice."

Analogy - using two things that have a similarity to make a case.

Analogy: "The human bra in is like a computer."

Chapter 14
Natural Language Has "Experience"

People need a language that has "experience". We need to know other people have lived all their lives talking in that language. We need to know that many centuries, many parents and their children, have made it work well. Natural language is always growing. The "closed system" of Globish, of course, is a beginning definition. Over time, Globish may add necessary words as *technical* or *international* when worldwide Globish speakers are using it.

The value of having a natural language is because it has been tested with many millions of people. Its most-used words have been turned over and over, like sand on a seaside, for centuries. These

第十四章
自然语言具有"经验"

人们需要一个具有"经验"的语言。我们需要知道别人一辈子都说那种语言。我们需要知道许多个世纪以来，很多父辈和他们的儿孙们已经把这点做得很好了。自然语言总在不断成长。当然，全球语的"封闭系统"是一个最初的定义。随着时间的推移，当全世界说全球语的人都在使用例如*技术性的*或*国际性的*词语的时候，全球语中就会加入这些必要的词汇。

拥有一门自然语言的价值在于它已被数百万人检验过了。几个世纪以来，这门语言中最常用的词汇就像海边的沙子一样被翻过来又翻过去。这些词汇

words are the *survivors* from all the natural languages that came into English. They are strong words, and useful words.

And these rules of Globish are not something someone just "thought up." For example, the way English deals with time through its verbs. Now all languages have different ways of communicating the order of happenings. But as much as any language, English-speakers have a proven language where events have relationships to each other in time. So timing is important to the English way of thinking, important to their communication. If they want to say something is happening "now" they use a continuous form, such as *I am reading this book*. That Present Continuous form means "exactly now." If they say *I read this book*, it means they have read it before now, are reading it now, and will continue to read it in the

作为所有自然语言的*幸存者*加入了英语词汇之中。它们是强势词语，也是有用的词语。

而且全球语的这些规则并不是某人刚刚"想出"的东西。例如，英语是通过它的动词来表达时间。如今所有的语言都有不同的方式来交流事件发生的顺序。但与其他任何语言相同的是，英语母语人士拥有一个经证实的语言，这门语言中的事件在时间上相互联系。因此，时间对于英语思维方式，对于他们的交流都很重要。如果他们想要说"现在"正在发生的事情，他们会用进行时，例如*我正在读这本书*。那么现在进行时就意味着"就是现在"。如果他们说*我读这本书*，这意味着他们之前在读这本书，现在正在读，而且将来会继续读它。

future.

These things are all important to a "way of thinking." They don't happen by someone's plan. Natural Language grows through trial-and-mistake-and-improvement, and that is why Natural Language works!

But why do we call Globish a "Closed System?" And is "closed" good?

所有这些东西对于一种"思维方式"来说都很重要。它们并不是因某人计划而发生的。自然语言的成长经历了尝试—错误—改进这样的过程，而这就是为什么自然语言能起作用！

但是我们为什么将全球语称之为一个"封闭系统"呢？那么"封闭"好吗？

Chapter 15
A Closed System: Globish Limitations

Closed Systems give us less to remember, and more to agree on

"Closed System" means we accept certain sets of limitations in what we are doing. It makes life easier when we agree to operate within those Closed Systems. We also have many other Closed Systems. Buses and trains and airplanes usually have places to step on and off. We usually drive on just one side of the road. Cars coming the other way stay on the other side, because it is a closed system. Otherwise, either side of the road would be OK, and there would be huge problems.

第十五章
一个封闭系统：全球语局限性

闭合系统让我们记忆的更少，而赞同的更多

"封闭系统"的意思是在我们做事情的时候受到某些特定的限制。当我们赞成在这个封闭系统内运行时，这就可以让我们的生活更加轻松。我们同样拥有许多其他的封闭系统。公交车，火车，和飞机通常都有可供上下的位置。通常我们只能在路的一边开车。从相反方向来的车在路的另一边，因为这是一个封闭系统。否则，如果去往同一方向的车在路的两边都可以开的话，那么就要出大问题了。

So…. why can't a language be a Closed System?

This is why Globish is most useful, as a Closed System, a language built on common limitations. You know what you have to learn, and can do so with less effort. And when you use it, you know all the rules that the other people know. It is based on reasonable limitations that non-native English speakers have when they use English. What we have been discussing in this book are main elements of that Closed System:

Globish is limited to 1500 words

Globish has limited ways of using words.

Globish has limited length sentences.

Globish is limited to understanding.

Globish has no limits in using hands, face, or body.

那么…为什么语言不能成为一个封闭系统？

这就是为什么全球语作为一个封闭系统是最有用的语言，它是建立在共同局限之上的。你知道你需要学习什么，而且可以付出较少的努力就可以做到。当你使用它的时候，你知道其他人了解的所有规则。这是以非英语母语人士使用英语时受到的合理局限为基础的。在这本书中我们一直讨论的是这个封闭系统的以下主要元素：

全球语的词汇不超过 1500 个

全球语的用词方法是有限的。

全球语句子的长度是有限的。

全球语只限于理解。

全球语在手臂，面部表情，或身体的使用上没有限制。

Chapter 16
1500 Basic Words

Before the English teachers all ask one question, let us answer it

There is *no* evidence that having 1500 words is ideal, except for one thing: *It's easier to learn 1500 words than 1800 or 2000 words.* And with fewer than 1000 words you won't have some very common words when you need them. Also, you can learn spelling and pronunciation of each individual word. That way you won't have to worry about a lot of spelling and pronunciation rules. (You probably already know that English doesn't do well with its spelling and pronunciation rules.)

These 1,500 words come from several lists of most-commonly used English

第十六章
1500 个基本词汇

在英语教师提出同一个问题之前，让我们来回答它

没有证据能够证明掌握 1500 个单词是最理想的，除了一件事情：*学习 1500 个单词要比学习 1800 个或 2000 个单词要更容易。*但词汇量少于 1000 的话，一些你需要的常用词将会不在其中。而且你还可以学习各个单词的拼写和发音。那样你就不需要担心大量的拼写和发音规则。（或许你已经知道英语的拼写和发音规则很复杂。）

这 1500 个单词来自数个最常用英语词汇表。它与美国之音

words. It is very much like the 1500 words used by Voice of America, but it has fewer political words. It is very much like basic Technical English used in international training books but without all of words for measurements. In fact, there are many lists of the "most common" 1500 words, and they all vary a lot in the last 200 words, depending on who is selecting. **So this is ours.**

所用的 1500 个单词非常相像，但政治词汇要少得多。它与国际培训书籍中使用的基本技术英语非常相似，但没有任何量度单位词汇。事实上，有很多词汇表包含"最常用的" 1500 个单词，但由于挑选单词的人不同，最后的 200 单词差异很大。**以下是我们的版本。**

The Basic 1500 Globish Words / 全球语 1500 个基本词汇

a = 一(个)	advertisement = 广告	alive = 活的	angle = 角度	arm = 手臂
able = 能够的	advise = 建议	all = 全部	announce = 公布	army = 军队
about = 大约，关于	affect = 影响	allow = 允许	another = 另外的	around = 周围
above = 上面的	afraid = 害怕	ally = 盟友	answer = 回答	arrest = 逮捕
accept = 接受	after = 后来	almost = 几乎	any = 任何	arrive = 到达
according (to) = 根据	again = 再次	alone = 单独的	apartment = 公寓	art = 艺术
account = 帐户	against = 相反	along = 沿着	apologize = 道歉	as = 同样地
accuse = 指责	age = 年龄	already = 已经	appeal = 上诉	ask = 询问
achieve = 完成	agency = 机构	also = 也	appear = 出现	assist = 帮助
across = 横过	ago = 以前	although = 虽然	apple = 苹果	at = -在
act = 行为	agree = 同意	always = 总是	apply = 申请	attach = 附加
adapt = 适应	ahead = 提前	among = 其中	appoint = 指定	attack = 攻击
add = 添加	aid = 援助	amount = 数量	approve = 批准	attempt = 试图
admit = 承认	aim = 目标	and = 和	area = 区域	attend = 出席
adult = 成人	air = 空气	anger = 愤怒	argue = 争论	attention = 注意

132

authority =权威	before =以前	body =身体	brush =刷	cause =原因
automatic =自动的	begin =开始	bomb =炸弹	budget =预算	celebrate =庆祝
autumn =秋季	behind =背后	bone =骨骼	build =建造	cell =细胞
available =可用的	believe =相信	bonus =奖金	bullet =子弹	center =中心
average =平均	bell =钟	book =书	burn =燃烧	century =世纪
avoid =避免	belong =属于	boot =靴子	burst =爆裂	ceremony =仪式
awake =唤醒	below =在下面	border =边界	bury =埋葬	certain =确定的
award =奖	bend =弯曲	born =天生的	business =商业	chain =链条
away =离去	beside =在旁边	borrow =借用	busy =忙碌的	chair =椅子
baby =婴儿	best =最好的	boss =老板	but =但是	chairman =主席
back =后面	betray =背叛	both =两者	butter =黄油	challenge =挑战
bad =坏的	better =更好的	bottle =瓶子	button =按钮	champion =冠军
bag =袋	between =之间	bottom =底部	buy =购买	chance =机会
balance =平衡	big =大的	box =盒子	by =通过	change =改变
ball =球	bill =帐单	boy =男孩	cabinet =内阁	channel =通道
ballot =投票	bird =鸟	boycott =抵制	call =呼叫	character =特色
ban =禁止	birth =出生	brain =脑子	calm =平静	charge =掌管
bank =银行	bit =少量	brake =刹车	camera =相机	chart =图表
bar =酒吧	bite =咬	branch =分支	camp =露营	chase =追逐
barrier =障碍	black =黑色	brave =勇敢	campaign =运动	cheap =便宜的
base =基础	blade =刀片	bread =面包	can =可以	check =检查
basket =篮子	blame =责备	break =打破	cancel =取消	cheer =欢呼
bath =沐浴	blank =空白	breathe =呼吸	capture =捕获	cheese =奶酪
battle =战斗	blanket =毛毯	brick =砖块	car =小汽车	chemical =化学的
be =是	bleed =流血	bridge =桥梁	card =卡片	chest =胸膛
bear =忍受	blind =瞎的	brief =简短	care =关心	chief =首领
beat =打击	block =块	bright =明亮的	carriage =客车厢	child =孩子
beauty =美丽	blood =血液	bring =带来	carry =携带	choose =选择
because =因为	blow =吹	broad =宽阔的	case =案例	church =教堂
become =变成	blue =蓝色	broadcast =广播	cash =现金	circle =圆圈
bed =床	board =木板	brother =兄弟	cat =猫	citizen =公民
beer =啤酒	boat =船	brown =褐色	catch =抓住	city =城市

civilian =平民　compete =竞争　court =法院　dear =亲爱的　differ =不同

claim =宣称　complete =完成　cover =覆盖　debate =辩论　difficult =困难

clash =冲突　compromise =妥协　cow =奶牛　debt =债务　dig =挖掘

class =类别　computer =计算机　crash =碰撞　decide =决定　dinner =晚餐

clean =干净的　concern =涉及　create =创造　declare =宣布　diplomat =外交官

clear =清楚的　condemn =谴责　credit =信用　decrease =减少　direct =直接

climate =气候　condition =条件　crew =全体人员　deep =深的　dirt =污垢

climb =攀登　conference =会议　crime =犯罪　defeat =打败　disappear =消失

clock =时钟　confirm =确认　crisis =危机　defend =捍卫　discover =发现

close =关闭　congratulate =祝贺　criteria =标准　define =定义　discuss =讨论

cloth = 布料　congress =议会　criticize =批评　degree =程度　disease =疾病

cloud =云雾　connect =连接　crop =农作物　delay =延迟　disk =圆盘

coal =煤炭　consider =考虑　cross =交叉　delicate =微妙的　dismiss =解散

coast =海岸　consumption =消费　crowd =人群　deliver =递送　dispute =争议

coat =外套　contact =联系　crush =压碎　demand =需求　distance =距离

code =代码　contain =包含　cry =哭泣　demonstrate =演示　divide =划分

cold =寒冷的　continent =大陆　culture =文化　denounce =谴责　do =做

collect =收集　continue =继续　cup =杯子　deny =否认　doctor =医生

college =学院　control =控制　cure =治愈　departure =出发　document =文件

colony =殖民地　cook =烹调　current =当前的　depend =依靠　dog =狗

color =颜色　cool =凉爽的　custom =风俗　deploy =部署　door =门

combine =结合　cooperate =合作　cut =切割　depression =沮丧　doubt =怀疑

come =来　copy =复制　damage =损害　describe =描述　down =向下

comfort =安慰　cork =软木塞　dance =舞蹈　desert* =沙漠　drain =排水

command =命令　corn =玉米　danger =危险　design =设计　draw =绘制

comment =评论　corner =角落　dark =黑暗的　desire =欲望　dream =梦想

committee =委员会　correct =正确的　date =日期　destroy =破坏　dress =礼服

common =普通的　cost =花费　daughter=女儿　detail =详情　drink =喝

communicate =沟通　cotton =棉花　day =白天　develop =发展　drive =驾驶

community =社区　count =计数　dead =死的　device =装置　drop =落下

company =公司　country =国家　deaf =的　die =死亡　drug =药物

compare =比较　course =课程　deal =处理, 交易　diet =饮食　dry =干燥的

during = 在…期间　enter = 进入　experiment = 实验　field = 领域　fool = 傻瓜

dust = 灰尘　entertain = 娱乐　expert = 专家　fierce = 猛烈的　foot = 脚

duty = 责任　environment = 环境　explain = 解释　fight = 打架　for = 为了

each = 每个　equal = 平等　explode = 爆炸　figure = 数字　forbid = 禁止

ear = 耳朵　equate = 等同　explore = 探索　file = 文件　force = 力量

early = 早的　equipment = 设备　export* = 出口　fill = 充满　foreign = 外国的

earn = 赚取　erase = 擦除　express = 表达　film = 电影　forest = 森林

earth = 地球　escape = 逃脱　extend = 延长　final = 最后的　forget = 忘记

east = 东方　especially = 特别　extra = 额外　finance = 金融　forgive = 原谅

easy = 容易的　establish = 建立　extreme = 极端　find = 找到　form = 形式

eat = 吃　estimate = 估计　eye = 眼睛　fine = 好的　former = 以前的

edge = 边缘　ethnic = 种族的　face = 脸部　finger = 手指　forward = 向前

education = 教育　evaporate = 蒸发　fact = 事实　finish = 完成　frame = 框架

effect = 效果　even = 甚至　factory = 工厂　fire = 火　free = 自由的

effort = 努力　event = 事件　fail = 失败　firm = 牢固的　freeze = 冻结

egg = 蛋　ever = 永远　fair = 公平的　first = 第一　fresh = 新鲜 de

either = 两者之中任一　every = 每个　fall = 落下　fish = 鱼　friend = 朋友

elastic = 有弹性的　evidence = 证据　false = 错误的　fist = 拳头　frighten = 吓唬

electricity = 电力　evil = 邪恶的　family = 家庭　fit = 适合　from = 来自

element = 元素　exact = 精确的　famous = 著名的　fix = 安装　front = 前面

else = 其他的　example = 例子　far = 遥远的　flag = 旗帜　fruit = 水果

embassy = 大使馆　except = 除…之外　fast = 快速的　flat = 平坦的　fuel = 燃料

emergency = 紧急情况　exchange = 交换　fat = 肥胖的　float = 漂浮　full = 满的

emotion = 情感　excuse = 借口　father = 父亲　floor = 地板　fun = 乐趣

employ = 聘用　execute = 例如　fear = 害怕　flow = 流动　future = 未来

empty = 空的　exercise = 练习　feather = 羽毛　flower = 花　gain = 获得

end = 末端　exist = 存在　feature = 特征　fluid = 液体　gallon = 加仑

enemy = 敌人　exit = 出口　feed = 喂养　fly = 飞翔　game = 游戏

enforce = 加强　expand = 扩大　feel = 感觉　fog = 雾　gang = 一伙

engine = 引擎　expect = 期待　female = 女性　fold = 折叠　garden = 花园

enjoy = 享受　expense = 费用　fertile = 肥沃的　follow = 跟随　gas = 气体

enough = 足够的　experience = 经验　few = 很少　food = 食物　gather = 收集

135

general = 一般	hang = 悬挂	holy = 神圣的	in = 在...之内	involve = 涉及
gentle = 温柔	happen = 发生	home = 家	inch = 英寸	iron = 铁
get = 获得	happy = 快乐的	honest = 诚实	incident = 事件	island = 岛屿
gift = 礼物	hard = 困难的，硬的	hope = 希望	include = 包括	issue = 问题
girl = 女孩	harm = 伤害	horrible = 可怕的	increase* = 增加	it = 它
give = 给予	hat = 帽子	horse = 马	independent = 独立的	item = 项目
glass = 玻璃	hate = 憎恨	hospital = 医院	indicate = 指出	jacket = 夹克
global = 全球的	have = 有	hostage = 人质	individual = 个人的	jail = 监狱
go = 去	he = 他	hostile = 敌对的	industry = 工业	jewel = 珠宝
goal = 目标	head = 头部	hot = 热的，辣的	infect = 感染	job = 工作
god = 上帝	heal = 治愈	hour = 小时	influence = 影响	join = 加入
gold = 黄金	health = 健康	house = 房子	inform = 通知	joint = 联合的
good = 良好的	hear = 听到	how = 怎样	inject = 注入	joke = 笑话
govern = 治理	heart = 心脏	however = 无论如何	injure = 损害	joy = 喜悦
grass = 草	heat = 热量	huge = 巨大的	innocent = 无辜的	judge = 判断
gray (grey) = 灰色	heavy = 沉重的	human = 人类	insane = 疯狂的	jump = 跳
great = 伟大的	help = 帮助	humor = 幽默	insect = 昆虫	jury = 陪审团
green = 绿色	her = 她	hunger = 饥饿	inspect = 检查	just = 刚刚
ground = 地面	here = 这里	hunt = 打猎	instead = 代替	keep = 保持
group = 组	hide = 隐藏	hurry = 匆忙	insult* = 侮辱	key = 钥匙
grow = 生长	high = 高的	hurt = 伤害	insurance = 保险	kick = 踢
guarantee = 保证	hijack = 劫持	husband = 丈夫	intelligence = 智力	kid = 小孩
guard = 守卫	hill = 山丘	I = 我	intense = 激烈	kill = 杀死
guess = 猜测	him = 他	ice = 冰	interest = 兴趣	kind = 种类
guide = 指导	hire = 雇用	idea = 想法	interfere = 干涉	king = 国王
guilty = 有罪的	his = 他的	identify = 识别	international = 国际的	kiss = 亲吻
gun = 枪支	history = 历史	if = 如果	into = 进入	kit = 成套的
guy = 家伙	hit = 打击	ill = 生病的	invade = 入侵	kitchen = 厨房
hair = 头发	hold = 持有	imagine = 想像	invent = 发明	knife = 刀
half = 一半	hole = 洞	import* = 进口	invest = 投资	know = 知道
halt = 停止	holiday = 假日	important = 重要的	investigate = 调查	labor = 劳动
hand = 手	hollow = 空心的	improve = 改善	invite = 邀请	laboratory = 实验室

lack =缺乏	lip = 嘴唇	march = 行军	minister =部长	nation = 民族
lake = 湖泊	liquid =液体	mark = 记号	minor = 次要的	native = 本国的
land = 陆地	list = 列表	market = 市场	miscellaneous =混杂的	navy = 海军
language =语言	listen = 听	marry =结婚	miss = 错过	near =附近的
large = 打的	little = 小的	master = 精通	mistake = 错误	necessary =必要
last =最后的	live = 活着	match = 相配	mix =混合	neck =颈部
late =晚的	load = 装载	material = 材料	mob = 暴徒	need =需要
laugh = 笑	loan =贷款	matter = 物质	model =模型	neighbor =邻居
law = 法律	local =本地的	may =可能	moderate = 适度的	neither =两者都不
lay =放置	locate = 位于	mayor =市长	modern = 现代的	nerve =神经
lead =领导	lock =锁	me = 我	money = 金钱	neutral = 中立的
leak =泄漏	log =日志	meal =餐食	month = 月	never = 从未
learn =学习	lone = 孤独的	mean = 意味着	moon = 月亮	new = 新的
least =最少的	long =长的	measure =措施	moral =道德的	news =新闻
leave =离开	look = 看	meat = 肉	more = 更多	next =下一个
left =左边	loose = 松散	media =媒体	morning = 早晨	nice = 美好的
leg = 腿	lose =失去	meet =遇见	most = 最多	night = 夜晚
legal =合法的	lot =很多	member =成员	mother = 母亲	no = 不
lend = 借给	loud =大声的	memory = 记忆	motion = 动作	noise = 噪音
length =长度	love = 爱	mental = 精神的	mountain = 山	noon = 中午
less =较少的	low =低的	mercy = 慈悲	mouth = 嘴	normal = 正常
let = 让	luck =运气	message =消息	move = 移动	north = 北方
letter = 信件	magic =魔术	metal =金属	much = 很，非常	nose = 鼻子
level =水平	mail =邮件	meter = 公尺	murder = 谋杀	not = 不
lie =说谎	main =主要的	method = 方法	muscle =肌肉	note = 笔记
life =生命	major = 专业	middle = 中间的	music = 音乐	nothing = 没有东西
lift = 举起	make =制造	might = 或许	must =必须	notice = 注意
light = 光	male =男性	mile =英里	my =我的	now = 现在
like =喜欢	man =男人	military =军事的	mystery = 神秘	nowhere = 无处
limit =限制	manufacture =制造	milk =牛奶	nail = 钉子，指甲	number = 号码
line = 线	many =许多	mind = 头脑	name = 名字	obey =服从
link = 连接	map =地图	mine =我的	narrow =狭窄的	object = 物体

observe =观察	own = 拥有	person = 人	potato = 土豆	public =公众
occupy =占据	page = 页	physical = 物理的	pound =英镑	publish =出版
occur =发生	pain =痛苦	pick = 拾取	pour =倾泻	pull = 拉
of = -属于	paint = 油漆	picture =图片	powder = 粉末	punish =惩罚
off = 脱离	pan = 平锅	piece = 件	power = 力量	purchase =购买
offensive = 冒犯的	pants =裤子	pig =猪	practice =实践	pure = 纯的
offer =提供	paper = 纸张	pilot =飞行员	praise =赞美	purpose =目的
office =办公室	parade =游行	pint =品脱	pray =祈祷	push = 推
officer = 官员	parcel =包裹	pipe = 管道	pregnant =怀孕	put =放置
often =经常	parent =家长	place =地点	present = 呈现	quality =质量
oil =油	parliament =议会	plain =平原	press = 按压	quart = 夸脱
old =老的	part =部分	plan = 计划	pretty =漂亮的	quarter =四分之一
on = -在…之上	party =聚会	plane =飞机	prevent =防止	queen =女王
once =一次	pass =通过	plant =植物	price =价格	question = 疑问
only =仅仅	passenger =乘客	plastic =塑料	print =打印	quick =快速
open =打开	past =过去	plate = 盘子	prison =监狱	quiet =安静的
operate =经营	paste = 张贴	play = 玩耍	private =私人	quit =退出
opinion =意见	path =路径	please = 请	prize = 奖	quite = 很
opportunity =机会	patient =病人	plenty = 很多	problem =问题	race =种族
opposite =相反	pattern =模式	pocket =口袋	process = 加工	radiation =辐射
oppress =压迫	pay = 支付	point = 要点	product =产品	raid = 突袭
or = 或者	peace = 和平	poison = 毒药	professor =教授	rail =铁路
order =命令	pen = 钢笔	policy =政策	profit =利润	rain =雨
organize =组织	pencil =铅笔	politics =政治	program =程序	raise =上升
other =其他	people =人们	pollute =污染	progress* =进展	range =范围
ounce =盎司	percent = 百分比	poor =贫穷的	project* =项目	rare =罕见
our =我们的	perfect = 完美	popular =流行的	property =财产	rate =比率
ours =我们的	perform = 表演	port =港口	propose = 提议	rather = 宁愿
oust = 撵走	perhaps = 或许	position =位置	protect =保护	ray =射线
out =外面的	period = 时期	possess =拥有	protest =抗议	reach =到达
over =上面的	permanent =永久的	possible =可能	prove =证明	react =反应
owe = 欠	permit =许可	postpone =推迟	provide =提供	read =阅读

ready =有准备的 responsible =负责 rule =规则
real = 真实的　rest =休息　run =跑
reason = 理由　restrain =抑制　sad =悲哀的
receive =接收　result =结果　safe =安全
recognize = 认出 retire =退休　sail =帆
record* =记录　return =返回　salt = 盐
recover =恢复　revolt = 反叛　same =相同的
red =红色　reward =奖励　sand = 沙子
reduce =减少　rice =米饭　satisfy = 满足
refugee =难民　rich =富有的　save = 拯救
refuse* = 垃圾　ride =骑　say =说
regret =遗憾　right =右边　scale =规模
regular =定期的 ring = 环　scare =惊吓
reject =拒绝　riot =骚乱　school =学校
relation =关系　rise =增加　science =科学
release =放松　risk =风险　score =得分
remain =保持　river =河　script =脚本
remember =记住 road =道路　sea = 海
remove = 移除　rob =抢劫　search =搜索
repair =修复　rock =岩石　season = 季节
repeat =重复　rocket =火箭　seat =座位
report =报告　roll = 滚动　second =第二
represent =代表 roof =屋顶　secret =秘密
request =请求　room =房间　section =部分
require =要求　root =根　security =安全
rescue =救援　rope =根　see = 看见
research =研究 rough =粗糙的　seed =种子
resign =辞职　round =圆的　seek =寻找
resist =抵制　row =行　seem =似乎
resolution =决议 rub =擦　seize =抓住
resource =资源　rubber =橡胶　seldom =很少
respect =尊重　ruin =毁灭　self = 自身

sell =出售　shop =店铺
senate =参议院 short =短的
send =发送　should =应该
sense = 感觉　shout =喊叫
sentence = 句子 show =显示
separate = 分离 shrink =收缩
series =系列　shut =关闭
serious =严重　sick = 有病的
serve =服务　side =旁边
set =设置　sign =标志
settle =定居　signal =信号
several =几个　silence =沉默
severe =严重的　silk =丝绸
sex =性别　silver =银
shade = 阴影　similar =类似
shake =动摇　simple =简单
shall = 应该　since =自从
shame =羞耻　sing =唱歌
shape =形状　single =单个
share =共享　sister =姐妹
sharp =锋利的　sit =坐
she = 她　situation =情况
sheet = 薄片　size = 尺寸
shelf =架子　skill =技能
shell = 壳　skin =皮肤
shelter =住所　skirt =裙子
shine =照耀　sky =天空
ship =舰　slave = 奴隶
shirt =衬衫　sleep =睡觉
shock =震惊　slide = 滑动
shoe = 鞋子　slip =滑
shoot = 射击　slow =慢的

139

small =小的	speech =演讲	story =故事	surprise =惊喜	than =比
smart = 聪明的	speed =速度	straight =直的	surround =环绕	thank =谢谢
smash =粉碎	spell = 拼写	strange =陌生的	survive =生存	that =那个
smell =气味	spend =花费	stream = 溪流	suspect =怀疑	the = 这个
smile =微笑	spirit =精神	street = 街道	suspend =暂停	theater = 剧院
smoke =烟雾	spot =斑点	stretch =伸开	swallow =燕子	their = 他们的
smooth =平滑的	spread =伸展	strike =罢工	swear =发誓	theirs = 他们的
snack =小吃	spring = 春天	string = 细绳	sweet =甜的	them = 他们
snake = 蛇	spy =间谍	strong =强壮的	swim =游泳	then =那时
sneeze =打喷嚏	square =广场	structure =结构	symbol =符号	theory =理论
snow = 雪	stage =阶段	struggle =斗争	sympathy =同情	there =那里
so = 因此	stairs =楼梯	study =研究	system =系统	these =这些
soap =肥皂	stamp =邮票	stupid =愚蠢的	table =桌子	they =他们
social =社会的	stand =站立	subject = 主题	tail = 尾巴	thick =厚的
society = 社会	star = 星星	substance =物质	take =拿	thin =薄的
soft = 柔软的	start = 开始	substitute = 代替	talk = 谈话	thing =事情
soil =土壤	starve =挨饿	succeed =成功	tall =高的	think =思考
soldier =士兵	state =状态	such =这种	target =目标	third =第三
solid = 坚固的	station = 车站	sudden =突然	task =任务	this =这个
solve =解决	status = 地位	suffer =受苦	taste =品尝	those =那些
some = 一些	stay =逗留	sugar = 糖	tax =税	though = 虽然
son = 儿子	steal =偷窃	suggest =建议	tea =茶	thought =想法
song =歌曲	steam =蒸汽	suit = 适合	teach =教	threaten =威胁
soon =很快	steel =钢铁	summer =夏天	team =团队	through =穿过
sorry =对不起	step = 脚步	sun =太阳	tear = 眼泪	throw = 扔
sort =分类	stick = 棍子	supervise =监督	tear =撕裂	thus =因而
soul = 灵魂	still =仍然	supply =供应	tell =告诉	tie =系，拴
sound =声音	stomach =胃	support =支持	term = 术语	tight =紧的
south =南	stone = 石头	suppose =假设	terrible =可怕的	time =时间
space =空间	stop =停止	suppress =压制	territory =领土	tin = 锡
speak = 说话	store = 储存	sure =当然	terror =恐怖	tiny = 微小的
special = 特别的	storm =风暴	surface =表面	test =测试	tire =轮胎

title =标题	tribe =部落	very = 非常	wear = 穿着	winter = 冬天
to =往，到	trick =把戏	veto = 否决权	weather = 天气	wire = 电线
today = 今天	trip =旅行	vicious =邪恶的	week = 星期	wise =英明的
together =一起	troop =部队	victim = 受害者	weight = 重量	wish = 祝愿
tomorrow =明天	trouble = 麻烦	victory = 胜利	welcome = 欢迎	with = 随着
tone = 音调	truck =卡车	view = 观看	well = 好	withdraw = 收回
tongue = 舌头	true = 真实的	violence = 暴力	west = 西	without = 没有
tonight =今晚	trust =信任	visit = 访问	wet = 湿的	woman = 女人
too = 也是	try =尝试	voice = 声音	what = 什么	wonder = 惊讶
tool =工具	tube = 管子	volume = 体积	wheat = 小麦	wood = 木头
tooth =牙齿	turn = 转动	vote = 投票	wheel = 轮子	wool = 羊毛
top =顶端	twice =两次	wage = 工资	when =何时	word = szó
total = 全部的	under =在…之下	wait = 等待	where = 哪里	work = munka
touch =触摸	understand =理解	walk = 步行	whether = 是否	world = 世界
toward =向	unit =单位	wall = 墙	which = 哪个	worry =担心
town =城镇	universe =宇宙	want = 想要	while =一会儿	worse =更坏的
track = 追踪	unless =除非	war = 战争	white = 白色	worth = 值得
trade =贸易	until =直到	warm = 温暖	who = 谁	wound = 受伤
tradition =传统	up =向上	warn = 警告	whole = 整个	wreck =残骸
traffic =交通	upon =在…之上	wash = 洗	why = 为什么	write = 写
train =火车	urge =敦促	waste = 浪费	wide = 宽的	wrong =错误的
transport* =交通	us =我们	watch = 观察	wife = 妻子	yard = 码
travel =旅行	use = 使用	water = 水	wild = 野性的	year = 年
treason = 叛国罪	valley = 山谷	wave = 波浪	will = 将会	yellow = 黄色
treasure =财宝	value = 价值	way =方式	win = 赢得	yes = 是的
treat =对待	vary =不同	we = 我们	wind = 风	yesterday = 昨天
treaty =条约	vegetable = 蔬菜	weak = 虚弱的	window =窗口	yet =然而
tree =树	vehicle = 车辆	wealth = 财富	wine = 葡萄酒	you = 你，您
trial =试验	version =版本	weapon = 武器	wing = 翅膀	young = 年轻的

When you learn a Globish word, you will not need to learn spelling rules or pronunciation rules. You will need to think of only that word. You should learn its individual pronunciation and how its individual spelling looks to you.

If you attempt to sound out every word from the English *spelling* **you will be sorry.** English writing has a very loose relationship with its sounds. But please...you must do everything to learn the **stressed** syllables in the Globish words. If you will say that stressed syllable in a **heavy** tone, most people can understand the rest.

One key sound that *is* more important to Globish - and English - than any other is the "*schwa*" sound. The *schwa* is almost not a sound. It usually "fills in" in words of more than one syllable, as a way of moving quickly over unstressed syllables. The *schwa* also makes trying to spell using sound very

当学习一个全球语单词的时候，你不需要学习拼写或发音规则。你所要想的就只是那个词。你应该学习它单独的发音以及在你看来它是如何拼写的。

如果你企图通过*拼*写来读出每个英语单词，那么**你会后悔的**。因为英语的书写与其发音之间的联系非常松散。但是请你必须尽你所能的学习全球语单词的**重读**音节。如果你用加强的语气读出一个词重读音节，那么大多数人都能理解剩余部分了。

对于全球语和英语来说，有个比其他任何发音更重要的关键音就是"中元音"。中元音几乎不是发音。它通常是对多音节单词进行"补充"，并作为一种快速读过非重读音节的方法。中元音也使得试图通过读音来

difficult.

All of these letters and letter-combinations will sound the same when an English speaker or a good Globish speaker says them. Using the schwa on the unstressed syllable is the most important thing about Globish (or English) pronunciation – and spelling – that you can know, because it makes everything else so much easier.

拼写一个词语变得非常困难。

当一个英语母语人士或全球语说得好的人读所有这些字母和字母组合时，发音会基本相同。对于全球语（或英语）的发音和拼写来说，使用中元音读出非重读音节是最重要的，到时你就会知道了，因为这会使其他所有事情变得如此轻松。

Chapter 17
When Globish Arrives

Since 2004, when the first books about Globish were published, the talk about Globish has changed. In that year, in forums on the Internet, many English teachers looked at the idea – and then looked away, saying: "I cannot imagine anything important being said in Globish" and "They are going to destroy our beautiful English language" and "Why can't they just learn how to speak decent English?" These forums are still on the Internet. You can Google them.

But many more people were still traveling from their countries, and still joining global businesses. Many more in this period were leaving their countries on work-permits for the first

第十七章
当全球语来临时

从 2004 年开始，当第一批关于全球语的书籍出版时，关于全球语的讨论改变了。在那一年，许多英语老师们在网上的论坛中看到了全球语，之后忽视了它，他们说："我不能想象用全球语能表达什么重要东西"；"他们将要破坏我们美丽的英语语言"；"他们为什么就不能学说一口地道的英语呢？"这些论坛如今仍然存在。你可以用谷歌搜索它们。

但是更多的人仍然不断的在他们的国家旅行着，仍然不断的加入国际商务中。在这期间更多的人第一次离开他们的祖国，拿着工作许可到更繁荣的

time to take jobs in more prosperous countries. They could not wait, they had to speak and be heard. And because they were speaking English across the world, more people began to see what these people with just "enough" English could really do. They built roads and houses, but many also made scientific discoveries and many more made lots of money in new worldwide businesses. All of this with just "enough" English.

Now, 5 years later, the tone toward Globish has changed. Most people now accept that native English speakers will not rule the world. Most people accept that there are important leaders who speak only "enough" English, but use it well to lead very well in the world.

So now there are very different questions, in the same forums. Some of the same people from 2004 are now asking:

"How many people now

国家就业。他们不能等，他们必须说话并让别人理解。然而正因为这些人在世界各地都说英语，越来越多的人开始观察这些只会说"足够的"英语的人能真正做些什么。这些人有的铺路盖房，但也有的做出了科学发现，还有更多人在新的世界贸易中赚了很多钱。所有这一切只需要"足够的"英语。

5 年后的现在，对于全球语的论调改变了。现在大多数人相信英语母语人士不会统治世界。大多数相信有些重要领导人只会说"足够的"英语，但却能够很好的运用它来很好的领导世界。

因此现在在同样的论坛中有了很多不同的问题。2004 年时的同样一些人现在问道：

"现在有多少人通晓足够的英

know enough English?"

"Should the native English-speaking teachers, who said 'you will never be good enough' now still be the guards over the language?" and

"Who will own the language?" And some few are beginning to ask: "How much English is enough?"

We think Globish – as described in this book – carries many of the answers.

Globish developed from observations and recording of what seemed to be the usual limitations of the average non-native speakers of English. Perhaps only 10% of those have studied English more than a year, or lived for a year in an English-speaking country. But they may have enough, if they know what *is* enough.

Perhaps in the next 5 years, more people will run out of money for never-ending

语？"

"那些说过'你将永远达不到足够好'的英语母语人士现在仍应是英语的守护者吗？"

"谁将拥有这种语言？"而且有些人开始问："多少英语才足够？"

我们认为全球语——正如本书中所描述的——承载着很多问题的答案。

通过对普通非英语母语人士常见的局限性进行观察和记录，从而发展出了全球语。或许这些人中只有 10%学习英语超过一年或在英语国家生活过一年。但是他们可能已经掌握了足够的英语，如果他们知道什么才是足够。

或许在接下来的 5 年里，越来越多的人会因为永无止尽的英

147

English classes. And more people will decide to follow careers and have families and … live…instead of always trying – year after year – for that goal of perfect English.

Globish may have their answer. And it may also have the answer for global companies who need enough English – but perhaps not perfect English – in their home offices and sales branches. Globish might work for these companies if their native speakers will -- at the same time -- learn how much English is too much.

Globish is what Toronto University linguist Jack Chambers called in 2009 "a new thing and very interesting…if (they are) formally codifying it, then Globish will gain status."

This book has been written not only to describe and codify, but to demonstrate Globish as a natural language, yet one that is in a closed system that is predictable and dependable,

语课程而花光所有的钱。而更多的人会决定创业并成家接着生活，而不是年复一年不停的尝试着达到完美英语的目标。

全球语或许就是他们的答案。而对于需要足够英语而不是完美英语的全球性公司来说，也可能有他们总部和销售分部需要的答案。如果这些公司的英语母语人士同时愿意学习多少英语算是太多，那么全球语对他们来说可能是有用的。

2009 年多伦多大学语言学家杰克•钱伯斯形容全球语："一个新事物而且非常有趣…如果（他们）正式将其系统化，那么全球语将获得地位。"

写这本书并不只是为了描述全球语并使其系统化，而是向人们展示处于一个封闭系统之中的全球语是一种自然语言，是可预测并且可靠的而且现在几

and is very close to being used across the globe now.

Then with so many good reasons for Globish that so many people agree with, why hasn't it happened? Why hasn't it arrived?

There seem to be 3 main barriers to that arrival:

Physical: People think they do not have the time or the money or the nearness to English Speaking to learn enough as a tool. With new media and Internet courses, this will make Globish all the easier to learn.

Language: Many English speakers truly feel that you cannot have just part of a language and you must always try for all of it. Quite a few language professors say that Globish is "not studied enough" or "not structured enough" – as always, without saying how much IS enough.

Political: The questions of

乎可以在全球使用了。

那既然这么多人因为如此多很好的理由而赞同全球语，为什么它还没有出现？为什么它还没有来临？

似乎有 3 个主要的障碍阻止它的来临：

物质方面：人们认为他们没有时间、金钱或不能经常练习英语口语，因此不能学习足够的量来将其作为工具使用。新媒体和网络课程使得学习全球语变得更加容易。

语言方面：许多英语母语人士真正的感受到你不能只学习一种语言的一部分而必须总是尝试掌握全部。相当多的语言教授们一如既往的说道全球语是"没有研究透彻"或"构造不完整"的，却没有说什么是透彻，多少是完整。

政治方面： 谁将使全球语成

149

who will make Globish happen, and who will require it, and who will finally "own" it seem central here. The remaining people who speak against Globish will discover that the citizens of the world will require it, make it happen, and own it – likely within the next 10 years. The very name *Globish* establishes this new point of view – that of the Global citizen who does not need the English past. This citizen needs only a dependable, usable language for the future.

Although it may not be historically exact, one has the image of the poor, beaten Englishmen who brought forth the Magna Carta in 1215. They were ruled by the foreign Normans, and the Normans wrote all the English laws in French, which the poor people in England could not understand. Along with others, these common people stood up before their Kings, at great risk to their families

为现实，谁需要它，以及谁将最终拥有它，这些问题似乎是才是焦点。很可能在接下来的 10 年中，余下的那些反对全球语的人会发现是世界的公民需要它，使之成为现实，并拥有它。全球语这个名字建立了这个新的观点：全球公民不再需要带有社会背景的英语。他们需要的只是一种未来可靠的，能用的语言。

虽然历史反映的可能没那么精确，但穷困潦倒的英国人在 1215 年签署了大宪章。当时他们被外来的诺曼人统治，而诺曼人给所有英国人制定的法律都是用法语书写的，英国的贫民看不懂这些法律。在他们自身及其家庭冒着巨大风险的情况下，这些普通的人们一同在他们的国王面前站了起来维

and themselves. And they said: "Enough!" They were frightened but still brave. Carrying only knives and clubs, they demanded that the laws by which they lived be more fair, and be given out in their own language – English.

Globish could be the interesting next step for the world...when people use English to be freed from the English. Globish will arrive when these common people from every country in the world, stand up and say "Enough." And Globish, as you see it here, will be there to give them...enough. When Globish arrives, you will talk to someone who just a few years ago could not understand you ...and turned away. And you will write in Globish to someone who understands and answers – perhaps even with a job or a good school possibility...Then you will look at these few words of Globish and say...

护自己的权力。他们说："够了！"虽然他们很害怕但仍然很勇敢。他们拿着刀子和棍棒，要求与他们生活息息相关的法律更加公平，而且要用他们自己的语言——英语来书写。

当人们使用从英语中解放出来的英语时，全世界令人关注的下一步有可能就是全球语。当这些来自世界上各个国家的普通人站起来说"够了！"的时候，全球语就会来临。而正如你现在看到的，那时全球语将会告诉他们多少算足够。当全球语来临时，你会与几年前听不懂你说什么而转身走开的人交谈。而且你会用全球语写信给能看懂的人，这个人给你回复时或许会向你提供一份工作或在学校教书的机会。那时你会看着这些全球语词汇感慨道：

"How rich I am.... Look at all of these words I have...So many words for so many opportunities and so many new friends...Look at all that I can do with them.... What valuable words they are...And I know them all!"

"我是多么地富有啊！看看我掌握的这些词汇...这么多词汇意味着同样多的机会与同样多的朋友...看看我能用它们做什么...它们是多么珍贵的词汇啊...而且我对它们了如指掌！"

globish

Appendix

附录

Synopsis

It would make very little sense to describe the details of Globish *either* to the person who has studied English -- or to the person who has not.

For that reason, we are giving only a synopsis of these chapters (Chapter 17-22) from the original book. The students who are studying English may, as their use of English -- or Globish -- improves, wish to try to read the original book. Their linguistic skills may then be ready for them to process that more specific information.

(In addition, this translated version will -- for obvious reasons -- leave out the adaptation from English to Globish of President Barack Obama's Inaguration Address of January 20, 2009.)

Chapter 17 (in the original book) - 1500 Basic Globish Words Father 5000

概要

无论将全球语的细节描述给学过英语的人或是没有学过英语的人，都是没有什么意义的。

因此，我们只将原书中的这些章节（第 17-22 章）做了如下概要。随着他们英语或全球语的进步，学习英语的学生们或许会想要阅读原文。那时他们的语言技能就可以处理更加具体的信息了。

（此外，显而易见的是此译本将省去用全球语改编的奥巴马总统于 2009 年 1 月 20 日发表的就职演说。）

第十七章（原文中）-全球语 1500 个基本词汇衍生出 5000

This chapter deals with how Globish -- and English -- is capable of making new words from basic words. There are basically 4 methods of making words from the basic 1500 words:

1. Putting two words together, as in: **class + room = classroom**

2. Adding letters to the front or the back of a word as in: **im + possible = impossible** (not possible) or **care + less = careless**. Many times it changes the part of speech, as when **care+less (careless)** becomes an adjective.

3. **Many** times the **same word** is used as a **noun,** a **verb,** and an **adjective. We drive a** *truck.* **With it, we** *truck* **vegetables to market. We may stop for lunch at a** *truck* **stop.**

4. Phrasal Verbs combine with prepositions to make different verbs, like: get up (in the

这一章讨论了全球语以及英语是如何能够用基本词汇构成新词的。从 1500 个基本词汇组成新词基本上有 4 种方法：

1. 两个词组合在一起，就像：
课+房间=教室

2. 在一个词的前面或后面添加字母，例如： **im + possible=impossible**（不可能）或 **care + less = careless**（粗心的）。多数情况下这会改变词性，正如 **care + less**（**careless**）变成了形容词。

3. **很多**时候同**一个词**可以作为**名词，动词，和形容词**来使用。**我们驾驶**货车。**我们用它将蔬菜**运到**市场里。我们可以在**货车停车场停**下来吃午饭。**

4. 动词短语和介词相结合成为不同的动词，例如：（早晨）

156

morning), take off (from the airport runway), or put up (weekend visitors in your extra room).

Chapter 18 (in the original book) - Cooking With Words

In addition to giving you enough words and ways to make more words easily, Globish uses **simple English grammar**, and avoids long and difficult sentences.

It stresses **Active Voice** sentences, but allows occasional **Passive Voice**. It uses the **Imperative** and the **Conditional** when necessary.

Globish uses **6 basic verb tenses** all the time -- the **Simple** and the **Continuous** for the **Present**, **Past**, and **Future** and four other verb tenses occasionally. **Different sentence forms** are used for **negatives**, and for various kinds of **questions**.

LEARNING TOOLS - *Globish IN Globish* is an interactive set

起床，（从机场跑道上）起飞，或（让周末访客在你家多余的房间里）过夜。

第十八章（原文中）-用词汇烹饪

除了教会你足够的词汇以及简便的构词方法之外，全球语使用的是简单英语语法，并且避免过长和困难的句子。

它强调**主动语态**的句子，但也允许偶尔使用**被动语态**。在必要的情况也可以使用**祈使句**和**条件句**。

全球语始终使用 6 种基本动词时态——一般现在时，一般过去时，一般将来时，现在进行时，过去进去时，和将来进行时。偶尔使用其它四种动词时态。**不同的**句式用于**否定句**和各种**疑问句**。

学习工具-*用全球语说的全球*

of Lessons in Globish at www.globish.com and many others will follow there.

Chapter 19 (in the original book) - Say "No" To Most Figurative Language

Idioms and Humor are the most difficult parts of a new language. Globish solves that problem by asking people to use very little of either. Idioms take hours -- sometimes -- to explain. Humor has not only language differences, but differences in culture and -- within culture -- ages and other backgrounds.

Chapter 20 (in the original book) - Globish "Best Practices"

Most of these are about people who know too much English for the needs and abilities of the largest group of people...those speaking Globish. So this chapter is about how a speaker must **take responsibility for the communication,** and do

*语*是 www.globish.com 网站中的一组全球语互动课程，而且该网站中还有许多其他课程。

第十九章（原文中）-对大多数比喻说"不"

习语和幽默是一种新语言中最难学习的部分。全球语的解决方法是让人们很少使用这两者。有时需要花费好几个小时解释习语的来龙去脉。幽默不仅因语言而不同，而且也会由于不同文化以及同一文化中的年龄和其他背景差异而不同。

第二十章（原文中）-全球语"最佳实践方法"

有些人掌握的英语已经超过了绝大部分说全球语的人的需求和能力，而这一章主要涉及这些人。因此本章的内容是关于一个说话者该怎样**对沟通负起**

whatever is necessary to communicate the message. This may mean: speaking or writing **in short sentences, listening for feedback** to make sure of understanding, and **using pictures or physical motions** to help the users understanding of words.

Chapter 21 (in the original book) - Critical Sounds for Global Understanding

This chapter is about pronunciation and the sounds various learners have trouble with. The aim is not to please the English speaker, but to make sounds that everyone can understand. This means concentrating on the most difficult ones, and making them acceptable. There are several other findings in this study, one being that learners do not have to have perfect sounds to be understood in Globish, but they do have to have the right stresses on parts of words, and they do need to know when to substitute with the "schwa" sound.

责任，以及怎样**不遗余力**的传递信息。这可能意味着：说写时**用简短的句子**，为确保对方理解要**听取反馈**，**使用图画或身体动作**帮助听众理解词语。

第二十一章（原文中）-全球语中的关键发音

这一章是关于许多学习者觉得苦恼的发音问题。我们的目的不是为了取悦英语母语人士，而是为了发出能让每个人都听懂的发音。这意味着要专注学习最困难的发音，并且要让它们能让人接受。在对这方面的研究中有一些其他的发现，其中的一个就是学习者们使用全球语时没有必要掌握完美的发音，但是他们必须将词语的重音读准，而且他们确实需要知道什么时候使用中元音过渡。

Chapter 22 (in the original book) - Globish in Texting

The Internet provides an environment that is excellent for Globish. Its messages are cut down to basics of English words because the messages are often charged by each little character over 160. So if love can become luv, u might save enough of ur money to visit the one u luv, just by shortening most words.

Texting is used in e-mails, chat sessions, instant messaging, and of course on mobile phones. Globish seems to have the perfect structures and numbers of words to be the text basis for people using the Internet.

第二十二章（原文中）-文字短信中的全球语

因特网为全球语提供了一个极好的环境。网上的短信被削减成基本的英语词汇，因为通常若短信超过 160 个字，那么超出部分就会按字数计费。因此如果 love（爱）可以变成 luv，那么 u（你）只需要缩短大多数词语就可以省下足够的钱去看望 u（你）luv（爱）的人。

人们会在电子邮件，网上聊天，即时通讯，当然，手机上用到文字短信。全球语似乎拥有完美的词汇结构以及词语数量供人们在网上发短信时使用。

Partial Resources

Council of Europe (2008).
Common European Framework of Reference for Languages: Learning, teaching, assessment. Retrieved http://www.coe.int/T/DG4/Por tfolio/?L=E&M=/main_pages/le vels.html , March, 17, 2009

Dlugosz, K. (2009) *English Sounds Critical to Global Understanding.* Pécs (Hungary): University of Pécs.

Graddol, D. (2006). *English Next.* London: British Council.

Nerrière, J. P. (2004). *Don't speak English. Parlez globish!* Paris: Eyrolles.

Nerrière, J. P., Bourgon, J., Dufresne, Ph. (2005) *Découvrez le Globish.* Paris: Eyrolles.

Other Sources

Jack Chambers, Toronto University linguist, as quoted in

部分参考资料

Council of Europe (2008).
Common European Framework of Reference for Languages: Learning, teaching, assessment. http://www.coe.int/T/DG4 /Portfolio/?L=E&M=/main_ pages/levels.html , 2009 年 3 月 17 日

Dlugosz, K. (2009) *English Sounds Critical to Global Understanding.* Pécs (Hungary): University of Pécs.

Graddol, D. (2006). *English Next.* London: British Council.

Nerrière, J. P. (2004). *Don't speak English. Parlez globish!* Paris: Eyrolles.

Nerrière, J. P., Bourgon, J., Dufresne, Ph. (2005) *Découvrez le Globish.* Paris: Eyrolles.

其他资料

杰克•钱伯斯，多伦多大学语言学家，摘自 "Parlez vous

"Parlez vous Globish? Probably, even if you don't know it," Lynda Hurst, Toronto Star, March 7, 2009

Notes of appreciation:

Dr. Liddy Nevile, of La Trobe University in Melbourne, and our friend in One Laptop Per Child, contributed moral support -- plus extensive editing which made this book a lot better.

Web Sites with Globish Information

www.jpn-globish.com - Original Globish site (much of it in French)

www.globish.com - New Globish portal site

www.bizeng.com (2008 series of business articles written in Globish by David Hon.)

Globish? Probably, even if you don't know it," Lynda Hurst，多伦多星报，2009 年 3 月 7 日

感谢：

来自墨尔本 La Trobe University 的 Liddy Nevile 博士以及我们一位在"每个孩子一台笔记本电脑"计划工作的朋友，他们给予了我们精神上的支持并帮助我们做了大量的编辑工作，使得本书变得更好。

包含全球语信息的网站

www.jpn-globish.com-最初的全球语网站（大多数文字是法语）

www.globish.com –新的全球语门户网站

www.bizeng.com （由大卫·洪用全球语编写的 2008 年系列商务文章）

Meet the Writers and the Translator

Jean-Paul Nerrière

As a vice-president of IBM Europe Middle East & Africa, Jean-Paul Nerrière was noted worldwide for his foresight in urging IBM to sell services instead of "selling iron". With IBM USA as a Vice President in charge of International Marketing, he was also using and observing English – daily – in its many variations. Nerrière's personal experience the world over enlightened him to a not-so-obvious solution to the global communication problem – *Globish*. Recently this has resulted in his best-selling books on *Globish* in French, Korean, Spanish and Italian, and the word Globish being known everywhere.

Nerrière has also been knighted with the *Légion d'honneur*, the highest award France can give.

认识一下作者和译者

让-保罗·内里埃

作为 IBM 分管欧洲，中东和非洲的副总裁，让-保罗·内里埃因其深谋远虑敦促 IBM 销售服务而不是"销售铁块"而闻名世界。在任职美国 IBM 负责国际市场销售的副总裁时，他每天都在使用并观察英语的许多种变体。内里埃周游世界的个人经历启发了他创造出不太明显的解决国际沟通问题的方案——全球语。最近的全球语法语版，韩语版，西班牙语版，以及意大利语版成为了最畅销书籍，而且全球语这个词也因此名声远扬。

内里埃也被授予了法国的最高荣誉"法国荣誉军团勋章"。

David Hon

As a young man, David Hon jumped off helicopters in Vietnam and taught English in South America. He had an MA in English and thought that someday he would write about English as an international communication tool. However, a different direction, into the computer age, led Hon to develop the world's first realistic medical simulators. He won international awards and created a successful company, Ixion, to produce those computerized simulators.

A short time back, he came upon Nerrière's Globish ideas, and Hon knew that this book *in Globish* was the one he had intended to write long ago. Voilà...

大卫·洪

年轻的时候，大卫·洪从越南战场的直升机上跳下，之后又去了南美教英语。他有一个英语硕士学位并且曾经想着某一天会写关于英语作为国际交流工具的文章。但是，计算机时代的到来将他引入了一个不同的方向，洪开发了世界上第一个现实医疗模拟人。他因此赢得的国际奖项并开办了一家成功的公司——Ixion，这家公司生产这些计算机控制的模拟人。

不久之前，他得知了内里埃的想法，而洪知道这本用全球语写的书就是他多年前想写的那本。就是这样...

Luo Xi

Born in Nanjing—capital city of six dynasties in history, Luo Xi grew up deeply involved in Chinese culture. At China's top foreign language university—Beijing Foreign Studies University he gained command of the English language and culture, and also the ability to teach it. During his college days, he taught English to people of many different ages, from 10 years old to 50. At one time he even gave English lessons in front of over 500 students in a summer camp.

Recently Luo Xi was one of the translators of an Indian TV series called Legend of Four Daughters which was broadcast by China's national TV station—CCTV. His current employment, in the international environment of modern Beijing, gives him daily insight on cultural differences between people he works with from various countries.

罗 希

罗希出生于六朝古都——南京，在他成长的过程中深深的受到了中国文化的熏陶。毕业于中国顶尖的外语大学——北京外国语大学，他掌握了英语语言及其文化，并能够教授英语。在大学期间，他曾教过从10岁到50岁之间许多不同年龄的人英语。他甚至还曾在一个夏令营中给超过500名的学生上英语课。近来罗希翻译了一部印度电视剧《四女奇缘》，这部电视剧曾在中国国家电视台——CCTV中播出。如今，他在当代北京的国际化环境中工作，这使他每天都能够洞察来自不同国家的同事们之间存在的文化差异。

21836572R00096

Made in the USA
Middletown, DE
12 July 2015